The Architecture of Value

Building Your Professional Practice

Craig Park

Copyright 2002, 2011 by **Craig Park.** All rights reserved. No part of this book may be used or reproduced in any manner without permission of the author, except in the case of brief quotations embodied in articles or reviews.

ISBN# 978-0-615-51334-8

Originally published as *Design. Market. Grow!* by SMPS, 2002. Excerpts and adaptations from Craig Park's bylined columns originally published by *Systems Contractor News* and the *SMPS Marketer* appear here with permission.

For more information, contact:
Craig Park
310.570.7636
craig@craigpark.com
www.craigpark.com

Published by:
Aquilan Press
Omaha, NE 68132
402.932.4065
www.aquilanpress.com

Book Design:
Craig Park

Cover Photo:
Walt Disney Concert Hall 2002
Craig Park

For Trevor

The Architecture of Value

TABLE OF CONTENTS

PREFACE	i
INTRODUCTION	v
PART I | **Design Your Practice:** *Think* Expertise	1
CHAPTER 1 | **Future**	7
CHAPTER 2 | **Strategy**	11
CHAPTER 3 | **Delivery**	19
CHAPTER 4 | **Leadership**	27
CHAPTER 5 | **Style**	33
CHAPTER 6 | **People**	39
CHAPTER 7 | **Knowledge**	43
CHAPTER 8 | **Innovation**	49
CHAPTER 9 | **Responsibility**	53
CHAPTER 10 | **Consultation**	57
CHAPTER 11 | **Collaboration**	61
CHAPTER 12 | **Synergy**	67
PART II | **Market Your Practice**: *Sell* Excellence	73
CHAPTER 13 | **Insight**	79
CHAPTER 14 | **Differentiation**	85
CHAPTER 15 | **Value**	91
CHAPTER 16 | **Interaction**	97

CHAPTER 17 | **Translation** 105
CHAPTER 18 | **Conversation** 109
CHAPTER 19 | **Economics** 117
CHAPTER 20 | **Identity** 121
CHAPTER 21 | **Referral** 127
CHAPTER 22 | **Network** 133
CHAPTER 23 | **Impact** 137
CHAPTER 24 | **Technology** 147
CHAPTER 25 | **Results** 159

PART III | Grow Your Practice: *Deliver* Experience 165
CHAPTER 26 | **Culture** 169
CHAPTER 27 | **Integrity** 173
CHAPTER 28 | **Management** 177
CHAPTER 29 | **Teamwork** 183
CHAPTER 30 | **Metrics** 187
CHAPTER 31 | **Opportunity** 193
CHAPTER 32 | **Agreement** 197
CHAPTER 33 | **Negotiation** 201
CHAPTER 34 | **Dialogue** 205
CHAPTER 35 | **Communication** 211
CHAPTER 36 | **Challenge** 217
CHAPTER 37 | **Evolution** 225
CHAPTER 38 | **Wisdom** 229

The Architecture of Value

AFTERWORD	235
ENDNOTES	237
BIBLIOGRAPHY	243
OTHER RECOMMENDED READING	247
INDEX TO WEB LINKS	249
ACKNOWLEDGEMENTS	253
ABOUT THE AUTHOR	255

PREFACE

*Things worthwhile generally do not just happen.
Luck is a fact, but it should not be a factor.
Good luck is what remains when intelligence and efforts
combine at their best. Luck is the residue of design.*
Branch Rickey

I ORIGINALLY WROTE THIS BOOK in 2002—published then by the Society for Marketing Professional Services (SMPS)—as *Design. Market. Grow!: Building Your Professional Service Firm through Expertise, Excellence & Experience.* In that first edition, I wrote of issues facing the professional service firms where I had worked and the best practices I discovered to address those issues.

In mid-decade, the book went through a second edition with minor changes and edits. In this third edition, I have completely updated, rewritten, and refocused the content to address the broader issues facing the professional service industry today. I have expanded the original writing by six chapters, and added significant new material.

Because of the book's focus on *lessons learned*, it became "recommended reading" for those studying the six domains of practice for the SMPS' Certified Professional Service Marketer (CPSM) accreditation.* I believe you will find it speaks equally to those whose focus is on leadership, management or operations.

---

* SMPS defines the six domains of a knowledge base for a certified professional as including: marketing research; marketing plan; client and business development; SOQs and proposals; promotional activity; and information, resource, and organizational management.

The Architecture of Value

I wrote this book specifically for leaders and aspiring leaders in the professional service market and that focus remains. You go to school to learn the *practice of the practice*, the "what" of our chosen path, but rarely are you taught the *business of the practice,* the "how" to turn that passion into a successful venture.

I have titled this new edition, *The Architecture of Value*™, which is the foundation for what will become *"The Architecture of..."* series; books related to all aspects of professional service including practice (*Value*), brand (*Image*), leadership (*Vision*), and technology (*Connection*), and their impact on the creation of a successful and enduring venture.

The fundamentals of creating an enduring professional practice parallel the practice of architecture (where collaborative teams conceive, design, and document a solution to a client's challenge, and coordinate in the execution of that solution: the build)—thus the new title for the book and the series. My goal is that this *Architecture of Practice*™ series becomes a useful tool and reference for professional service firms.

I have worked in the building industry for more than 40 years. I served for many years in roles of project manager, principal-in-charge, and operational management. I have held senior roles in marketing, business development, and strategic planning for consultative, integration, and manufacturing companies, culminating in the position of Chief Marketing Officer (CMO) with two major architectural firms.

This integrated experience focused my attention on client service and organized process. While written from a building-industry consultant's perspective, I believe the need for creating, growing, practicing, and sustaining a professional service firm is common to all other service-oriented businesses as well.

Preface

The lawyer, doctor, advertising agency, accountant, or financial advisor each need to create, advance, and build their practice based on the creativity their expertise and experience affords and the result their clients will have from working with them.

My writing often references "designer," "consultant," "building," "integrator," and "contractor" in the context of seeing an advisory effort from concept to fruition. For those not in the building industry, think of those terms as metaphors for the different roles needed in your practice to see your advice implemented.

I should also note that I often speak of the goal of building a profitable business. However, profit is not a *strategy* that I espouse. Profit is the *result* of creating, marketing, and delivering quality service. Businesses created only for making money seldom endure. Those organizations that focus on client-centric value delivery are those that last.

At the time of the book's original publication, we were just coming out of a serious recession caused, by most accounts, by the dot-com crash. This recession was further complicated by the aftermath effects of the 9/11 tragedies. When I started writing the original manuscript in the mid-1990s, we had also seen a steep rise in the economy—as measured by the Gross Domestic Product (GDP) and stock market indices—caused again by the growth that came from that same technologically driven innovation.

Today, we are at the end or in the midst of—depending on your point of view—a similar but widely acknowledged deep recession. Another round of economic growth resulting from, by most accounts, the exploitation of financial derivatives based on unsecured home mortgages, and complicated by the ongoing military actions in the

The Architecture of Value

Middle East caused this recent downturn. These events produced a major reset in the way we look at both the present and the future.

As a result, my concept of *value* has become even more critical to the future of any professional service practice. Much of my writing then, as now, relates to creating, establishing, and sustaining a professional practice, and focuses on weathering uncertainty.

Many have called today's socio-political-economic reality 'the new normal.' I would postulate that we are at the beginning of a new cycle, one that will bring about a seachange in the professional service industry. The rise of real-time, on-line, multi-dimensional collaboration, telepresence, and social media-driven information exchange will forever alter the profession, regardless of your market or area of expertise.

THE OPPORTUNITY TO LEVERAGE THIS TRANSFORMATION motivated me to write *The Architecture of Value*. I hope you will find reading this new edition as worthwhile as the first.

INTRODUCTION

> *Whatever you do or dream you can do—begin it.*
> *Boldness has genius and power and magic in it.*
> Johann Wolfgang Von Goethe

THROUGHOUT MY CAREER, I have been on a quest. Intrigued by the ways in which professional services define their business models, I looked closely at how we provide value to our clients. My personal goal is to seek out and explore new paradigms, looking for practical ways to build the new, profitable, and lasting service venture.

I believe, at a baseline, the contemporary professional service practice must provide cost control, project accountability, and speed of delivery. These are the simple metrics for success in any professional service.

This means you must have an unerring focus on sustained profitability, responsibility to the client, and improve time-to-market for both you and for your clients—cheaper, but still profitable, better, and faster!

In this book, I share from my experience and study some directions on how you can develop those characteristics in yourself, your staff, and your practice.

THE PREMISE

I have organized this book around three sets of three: three simple goals: *think, sell,* and *deliver*; three simple actions: *design, market, and grow*; and, three overarching themes: *expertise, excellence, and experience.* I draw my observations and lessons learned from more than 40 years of experience in the building industry.

I framed them as practical directions for leaders and aspiring leaders, sharing real-world examples on how to build a professional service firm through a combination of learning, leadership, collaboration, and values—the basis for a successful and enduring practice.

The Architecture of Value

Fundamentally, every professional service is founded on the ability to *think* (ideation), *sell* (provide valued worth), and *deliver* (as a brand promise). Further, by developing a practice that has a *design*—a strategy, a vision, and a path based on your *expertise*, you are taking the right first step. To *market* is equally important. When based on the firm's *excellence*, it is another step toward success. Finally, to *grow* comes from the right practice of your practice—providing work that people love to do, and as a result, that clients love to *experience* (and return for more).

I am not promoting only growth in size, though that too may be part of your design. Many practices desire to remain small. My focus here is on growth in profitability because in the end, the bottom line will govern your ability to sustain and endure.

Although steeped in my experience in the design, construction, and technology sectors, I believe these best practices directly apply to any other knowledge-based advisory service business, including legal, finance, technology, or management consultancy. These are the best practices for any enduring business. When used every day, they will help you succeed.

To be truly effective, the professional service firm must leverage its *expertise*. A practice designed around truly advisory knowledge-based consultative expertise determines and satisfies each client's unique needs. The firm's efforts in the market must focus on *excellence*. This quality differentiates the best from the commonplace. Finally, the practice must provide *experience*—such a positive experience both internally and externally that it draws staff to want to help it grow, and it brings the client back for more.

As you read this book, it will become increasingly clear that a third set of three outcomes—*value, image, and vision*—are also very important elements in my premise. I believe they transcend all enduring companies and are essential to the successful professional service

Introduction

practice in the future. *Value* to both the firm and the client should be the foundation of the practice. *Image* (and recognition of your base identity) is the brand message that great firms communicate. *Vision* reflects your leadership—on all levels within and outside your practice—and is the core competency of success.

These three outcomes are complemented by a forth separate, but related outcome—*Connection*—that acknowledges the impact technology has had on the work we do, the way we communicate, and the way we interact with our clients.

A SMALL CAUTION

Throughout the book, I have provided anecdotal stories under a sidebar subtitled "PERSPECTIVE." In these snippets, I share a personal story related to the topic at hand. Positive or negative, these lessons learned, more often than not, led to increased knowledge (and sometimes wisdom), if not greater caution. My hope is that some of what I have faced, learned, and shared here helps you build an enduring practice of your own.

Unfortunately, as in life, not everything goes the way you plan. In writing a book with a goal of providing positive reinforcement for the best practices to which you should aspire, I found myself reflecting on the darker side of some of my experiences. I have included those thoughts as well.

Words like exaggerate, excess, exclude, excuse, extraneous, and extravagant often describe the results from the lesser character and practice flaws of the most well meaning people and organizations. However, I know you can transcend these factors in the search for higher value and wisdom.

Therefore, I conclude the book with a cautionary parable, based on real experiences—told honestly, but with just a tinge of sarcasm. Irony and satire can be doors to new awareness. My hope is this parable will

The Architecture of Value

remind you of the virtues of teamwork, the values of mindfulness and awareness, and the benefits of communication.

A LITTLE BACKGROUND

I am an architect by training, a technology consultant by many years of practice, a marketing strategist by passion, and a business leader by just a little of Branch Rickey's definition for luck.

I have had the pleasure of working with great clients, great teams, and great building projects; the kind of experience business strategist, Tom Peters regularly describes so simply and eloquently as *"WOW."* Nevertheless, I have also shared the pain of miserable clients, fractious teams, and misguided projects. Fortunately, the former have far outweighed and outnumbered the latter.

As I learned more, I focused my thinking on finding practical ways the service firm can improve proficiency, responsiveness, cost performance, scalability, and results. I became a convert to the value of multi-disciplinary collaboration. I believe this will lead to more satisfied clients and, as a result, an enduring practice. I have included much of what I have learned about that along the way herein.

A voracious reader, I try to absorb and integrate the best thinking from both within and outside the building industry. I have included many insights and examples drawn from thought leaders related to building a successful professional practice. I respect their ideas and that apply them to the issues I raise.

Throughout the book, I provide footnotes to define terms, and endnotes to attributed sources, and conclude with a bibliography of referenced and recommended reading, as well as an index of web-references for listed companies, periodicals, and people of interest,.

My hope is that I might motivate you to look beyond the status quo and reliance on conventional wisdom. Seek out and find new thought-provoking resources that will help you reach your own awareness of

Introduction

possibility. I also hope you will find my own observations and lessons learned helpful as you pursue your own quest to build an enduring professional service practice.

The message I want to convey is that the combined actions of thinking, selling, and delivering, by designing, marketing, and growing, will ultimately allow you to master your expertise, leverage your excellence, and convey the kind of positive experience that is truly beneficial to both your clients' goals and your practice.

I BELIEVE THE RESULTS AND REWARDS for this focus will enable your practice to become truly enduring—a practice about which your clients exalt you exponentially and exuberantly with positive words like exactly, exciting, exemplary, and extraordinary!

The Architecture of Value

PART I | Design Your Practice: *Think* Expertise

Design is the only difference that matters.
Mark Dziersk

EXPERTISE CREATES THE OPPORTUNITY to build a professional service practice that has a design—one that has a vision, a mission, and workable strategies. In the beginning, base expertise on your own unique talents combined with those of your associates and staff.

Professional mastery is the hallmark of enduring companies. From the first creative idea, through the quest for ongoing continual learning, the focus of a lasting practice is on shared knowledge. An expertise-driven practice provides definable benefits. You differentiate from your competitors as a result. Moreover, your practice proves its worthiness by growing beyond expectations.

The elements that define the meaning and application of expertise are many. The first step is an analysis of strategy, leadership, and style that will define the culture of your firm. Most companies procrastinate on this point. That is human nature. However, in today's rapidly evolving economic climate, it is an imperative.

Next, you must decide what kind of work your practice will deliver, and learn ways to find new knowledge and foster innovation. You must also learn to recognize the evolutionary factors that will change your business over time. Again, most firms do not age very well. The tar pits of business are full of examples. Just look at now defunct blue chip companies like Digital and Montgomery Ward from a decade ago, Borders and Lehman Brothers from more recent times. The list of professional service firms that have disappeared is much longer.

Finally, the success of the practice comes down to recognition of the importance of collaboration, the responsibility that comes with expertise, and the value that true advisory services bring to market.

The Architecture of Value

FUTURE
We enter the second decade of the 21st century with a new perspective. The future is not clear. The resiliency of the economy is in question. The value of consultative services, as perceived by many clients, is waning. However, the ability—enabled by advances in communication technology—to create effective, collaborative interactions bodes great promise. For professional services, this is a time for redefining value and for delivering client-centric solutions.

STRATEGY
Building an effective strategy for your business is a function of metrics. By setting goals and objectives that are measurable, you can mark your progress. Also important is process. Understanding service delivery methods and determining those that work best for you, allows you to provide appropriate and profitable service. Equally important is communication. Developing a culture built on shared values and open dialogue, both internally and externally, you foster interaction, creativity, and innovation. Strategy becomes the foundation upon which your expertise can be of true value.

DELIVERY
One of the first things necessary in designing your firm is developing a focus on the kind of service you will deliver. Traditional consultative and implementation efforts follow the prime design/sub-consultant or prime contractor/subcontractor models. You can pick your role from these old models, or adapt a more forward thinking and collaborative structure. New practice models provide alternative business opportunities and the potential for greater profitability. Awareness of client perspectives on value and delivery remain key, however your business manifests.

Design Your Practice

LEADERSHIP
Understanding the elements of effective leadership and committing to continual development of personal professional development is critical to ongoing success. Expertise evolves with experience. Leadership develops as you master your craft, and begins to guide and mentor those around you with your vision. Leadership transcends the definition, marketing, and growth of your practice. The single element of leadership combines expertise, excellence, and experience.

STYLE
Your personal style is often defined by one of several personal profiling systems like Meyers-Briggs, colorgenics, DISC-theory, or the Hippocratic temperaments These are but a few of many popular character-mapping systems It is important to learn which mode you favor and to recognize the modes of others. Varieties of archetypes also define your style of leadership. Learning and developing your particular style—and recognizing the styles of your peers, your staff, and your clients—are important steps in developing and applying your expertise effectively internally and externally.

PEOPLE
Designing the work environment in ways that emphasize and support your values and enable its people to grow is one of the keystones of long-term success. Recognizing the benefits of mentoring, coaching, and training, while providing an interesting and fun environment in which to work, goes a long way to foster loyalty. A workplace that engages the spirit and soul of the staff engages the spirit and soul of your clients.

KNOWLEDGE
When do you know that you do not know? Can you design your practice without research or thought about future possibilities? Can you grow without finding what contributes to your clients' business success? Can

The Architecture of Value

you succeed without seeking new ways to improve client service? Building your practice will happen with a few missteps along the way. Learning from others is often as valuable as developing your own expertise when you *"learn by doing."*[†] Finding sources for that learning is a key element to continual improvement of your expertise.

INNOVATION
To build a profitable and creative organization that fosters imagination, inventiveness, and ingenuity requires new paradigms. That shared expertise combines to provide a basis for excellence and experience. Building a business that embraces innovation as one of its cornerstones can yield both fun and profit growth.

RESPONSIBILITY
Establishing a culture of personal responsibility is important. Demonstrating personal responsibility establishes that collaboration, measurable criteria, and innovative solutions are the norm. Responsibility focuses your expertise on your clients' needs. Responsibility provides benefits to your clients' projects by contributing to their own success.

CONSULTATION
A well-designed practice provides relevant advisory services based on expertise. Expert counsel is the currency of this age of collaboration. Master your expertise, and you can leverage your intellectual property. Build trust with your clients, and you can profit from this new value proposition for the building industry.

COLLABORATION

[†] The academic philosophy practiced at my alma mater, California Polytechnic State University in San Luis Obispo. It blends theory and practice; ensuring graduates are ready to bring their skills to work effectively on day one.

Design Your Practice

The demand for improved service delivery puts emphasis on the importance of multi-disciplinary expert collaboration. Clients seek the combined expertise of the team. Developing mutual respect of the knowledge of others is the hallmark of the enduring practice. Designing the strategies, developing leadership, building culture, and providing service are the key factors in how you think about your practice.

SYNERGY

Collaboration is a theme I repeat throughout this book. I believe collaboration defines success in the professional service industry. While there is much talk on the subject, there remains a tendency to try to do everything for a client, without the aid of a collaborative effort. However, collaboration leads to new opportunities. Disparate cultures that share resources and learning continue to expand and enhance their businesses, while delivering new and innovative solutions to their clients' challenges.

THE FOLLOWING CHAPTERS DEFINE each of these elements of expertise critical, which if executed effectively, can lead to the success of your professional practice.

The Architecture of Value

CHAPTER 1 | Future

The most radical... transformation would occur simply if everybody truly evolved to a mature, rational, and responsible ego, capable of freely participating in the open exchange of mutual self-esteem.
Ken Wilber

INTEGRATING THREE IMPORTANT ELEMENTS of the social environment—*science, morals,* and *art*—should be your goal in creating a truly optimal professional practice.[1] You can use this model for a professional service firm's practice by seeing each of these elements characterized as *truth, good,* and *beauty,* where:

- **Leadership** (management/finance/IT/HR) represents the science—they create *truth* about an organization—defining its "vision" by thinking expertise.

- **Communication** (marketing/business development/PR) represents the morals—they tell the *good* of an organization—defining its "brand" and selling excellence.

- **Project Delivery** (design/operations) represents the art—they show the beauty of an organization, internally and externally—defining its "value" and delivering experience.

I believe the key to the practice of the future is recognizing the importance of all three elements in creating the sustainable professional service firm. An integral practice has further development potential in the individual, cultural, behavioral, and social spectrums. It is not just the awareness and acknowledgement of the importance of three core elements of science, morals, and art.

In the future, the successful firm will be committed to individual and organizational development along the lines of the four spectrums to truly create a differentiated value proposition and enable the optimized service delivery.

The Architecture of Value

AVOIDING SILOS
Unfortunately, and too often, silos are created to protect the interests of these three elements (and sometimes their component parts), which work against to any attempt to create an integral approach for the firm. Once created for geographic or functional reasons, these silos are very difficult to span. They work at odds with individual and organizational development, unfortunately but naturally, being self-protective.

The key is to make sure that any endeavor is touching all the bases when it comes to various problems and their solutions. Complex problems demand a comprehensive approach to their solution. Beyond technical competence, those solutions must combine systems theory with emotional intelligence and the impact of and on your culture.[2]

Only when you truly and fully integrate the three core elements of leadership, communication, and project delivery will you have the fundamental framework for an enduring practice. Responsible practitioners understand, respect, and support each other. They can adapt to the inevitable economic, political, and social changes. They have a continual impact on the evolution of professional service.

One only has to look at the sweeping impact of the financial crisis that began in 2008, which will have a significant impact on all aspects of your life for many years to come. During the past few years, many firms *hunkered down* to try to weather the storm. Few developed the integral practice approach that may have anticipated and planned for the impact of radical change, and are now prepared to not only continue, but to grow, through these difficult times.

CONCISE COMMUNICATION
Professional service firms provide value based on applying expert knowledge in practice areas that are not typically in the core competency of the hiring client's organization. That is the driving factor for the engagement—providing advice and counsel that addresses an

Future

unknown or technical challenge that is having a negative impact on client's goals.

Accountants, architects, design consultants, engineers, financiers, management consultants, organizational development consultants, and technology advisors each add value in developing solutions to facilities, economic, personnel, or communication issues facing their client.

Each of these professions comes with a vocabulary unique to their practice. The best translate their expertise into terminology and supporting explanatory communication that illuminates the issue at hand, in language easily understood and applied. True professionals in these areas of practice become trusted advisors and enjoy long-term relationships that broaden and deepen over time. The worst hide behind esoteric acronyms and obtuse language that masks real advice.

Those advisors who provide clear, concise data, analysis, and pragmatic (both strategic and tactical) recommendations build business. Those that do more than just consult—who provide support for the solution—will increase their repeat and referral business.

Those who do not—and continue to use mind-numbing phraseology like *"leverage integrated massive-aggressive strategies that lead to the logical evolution of exceptional results"* —will burn and churn through their clients. Be the former. Avoid the latter.

FUTURE THINKING

The practice of the future will develop integral vocabulary, dialogue, and delivery methods that do not compromise on leadership, communication, or project delivery. As a result, they satisfy your clients' demand for effectiveness (*expertise*), quality of service (*excellence*), and timeliness (*experience*).

Reaching a level of communication, collaboration, and connection with your clients that recognizes their goals, truly informs and enables their decision-making processes, and achieves a mutual understanding of

The Architecture of Value

measurable results is the key to competitive differentiation and ultimate practice success.

The practice of the future will be less about iconic results. It will be more concerned with extending a growing cultural awareness. It will engage and address the societal impact of its solutions. The practice of the future will consciously seek to develop a physical manifestation that is good, true, and beautiful.

Proficiency in the latest technological advances, such as building information modeling (BIM) in the construction sector, is important. Creating expertise in a market niche can focus the efforts of your firm, but may be risky if demands change. Innovation will move your practice in more socially appropriate directions.

New service delivery models and alternate team structures are the evolution of the practice of the practice. Integrated project delivery, connecting owner, consultant, and implementer in a truly collaborative business relationship is the next progression of the practice.

At the end of the day, it is how you deliver vision (science; the true), value (morals; the good) and create your brand (art; the beautiful) through your own leadership, communication, and project delivery teams that will define the integral practice of the future.

CHAPTER 2 | Strategy

The great architect of the universe never builds a stairway that leads nowhere.
Robert A. Millikan

EXPERTISE IS THE FOUNDATION of the professional service practice. In a classic business model, developing a success strategy is a matter of positioning. First, based on your expertise, you find a unique place in the market where you can generate revenue. Then you work to distinguish the unique qualities of your services and erect barriers-to-entry for your competitors. Finally, you develop and refine your competencies. The processes that renew and expand your expertise reinforce your position in the marketplace.

The results: your profits grow and grow. Sounds simple, but in reality, the suddenness with which local, regional, national, or global economic dynamics change poses a serious dilemma. Do you stick to your predetermined goals, or opt for reactive and situational change of direction? The answer is to include the dynamics of change in your strategic planning process.

Building a solid strategy is the first step to designing an enduring practice. One overriding problem with traditional strategic planning is the source of direction. When developed solely by management, strategic initiatives usually fail. When developed through input from all levels of the organization, successful strategies reflect the best practices of the people who are responsible where the rubber meets the road.

A strategic plan answers two important questions: *"Where do you want to go?"* and, *"How do you want to get there?"* In a stable market economy, the emphasis should be on the where. In a dynamically changing market, the how becomes much more important. The key is to keep it simple and measurable. By developing a plan that has definable

The Architecture of Value

steps and metrics, you can easily monitor both progress and the impact of change on the plan's goals.

Develop a few simple strategies. Pay attention to the pulse of the marketplace—especially to that of your clients and your clients' clients—to gain a competitive advantage. Focusing on your core competencies and expanding services only when they enhance the basic deliverable will give you a valuable advantage.

The key element of a successful strategic plan is its founding principle. The strategic principle is a tangible statement, grounded in fiscal reality, which defines the direction in which you want your company to go. It is neither a mission statement nor a visionary aspiration. The strategic principle functions as a metric that helps you decide which opportunities to pursue and which to forgo.

For example, if you decide to focus on being the local, regional, or national market leader in a client sector, you will be less likely to waste time pursuing opportunities in other, non-relevant sectors. Again, this may seem like common sense, but too often firms forget their core goals. In search of the grail of profit, they erroneously and ineffectively pursue high-dollar opportunities outside their ability, or they do not anticipate economic changes.

> **PERSPECTIVE**
> At one point in my career, I joined a large, well established, and by all accounts, successful design and engineering firm as the senior marketing executive. However, while the company regularly created annual business plans and budgets for their operating units (which parenthetically, annually collected dust on several bookshelves), they had no overarching corporate strategic plan, nor did they communicate the individual business plans with each other.

Strategy

When I inquired about a corporate strategy, I was encouraged to "create one." Empowered, I organized and facilitated the firm's first overarching strategic planning effort, which ultimately became the annual model for each operating unit's business plan as well.

The plan included input from senior executives in the "C-Suite" of leadership, operations, finance, human resources, marketing, and information technology. The plan defined department and individual goals and responsibilities, and established measurements to gauge progress. We reviewed these metrics on quarterly basis. We adjusted the plan based on the "current reality" of the economic climates.

As a result, the plan was concise (reduced to one binder), focused, and easily communicated. We shared the plan with the firm's leadership and business unit managers, and posted it on the firm's intranet for every staff member to read and review.

This approach to planning became the template for the business units, and established a long-term (strategic), mid-term (business), and short-term (action) goals, and processes that is now used throughout the organization.

MEASURES OF SUCCESS

View the strategic plan as analogous to a set of construction plans. It should be clear and understandable to all levels of the craftspeople (your staff) necessary to build it. The objective should be visible and visionary to the buyer (your clients). The results should be a successful venture, satisfying to both (and to your stakeholders). When looking at your firm's strategy, ask yourself, *"Is it real? Can I build it?"* If the answer is yes, more often than not, *"They (the clients) will come."*

The Architecture of Value

Too often, firms develop a lofty (and nebulous) goal as the foundation for their strategy, like *"We want to be the best in class!"* Worse, many firms have no defined plan. They work with amorphous goals that change on a whim of their leadership.

Strategies based on solid market-based metrics are good, as are goals based on specific profitability measures. You need other metrics to reach those goals. How many employees will it take to meet your goal? What new services will you need to offer? What technologies do you need to support your services? What other resources will you need?

Underlying any strategy is the value proposition that you offer to your clients. These can be design, innovation, cost-savings, or high reliability, among many others. These core values define your approach to client service. In the end, those values will be the basis for repeat and referral work, and more profitability. However, the value proposition must be bi-directional. True value engages and satisfies the buyer, while meeting the goals of the seller.

THE PLANNING PROCESS

In the global marketplace, with a significant level of insecurity as a major component, developing a long-range plan requires new insights. Most firms try to predict what the marketplace will be like in three to five years, and then use those predictions as the basis for developing their strategies. This approach is important, but reliance on a single planning model can be ruinous if you are wrong. All plans should include an element of evolutionary change.

The uncertainties of recent times—a recessionary downturn combined with the fears associated with potential physical threats to people, buildings, and infrastructure—emphasize the importance of developing various scenarios as part of your strategic plan. Look at the world in this new light and it changes everything.

Strategy

By developing a strategic plan that includes the implications of where you locate your business, where your clients are located, and whom you hire, helps mitigate the impact of revolutionary change. Factoring contingencies for major upheaval in your business, and in the business of your client, is now more than ever a part of *"business as usual."*

Designing systems and processes that engage all levels of your organization in the economics of project delivery is an excellent way to analyze how to improve your overall strategies. Focusing on core competencies and core markets may mean divesting some operations, staff, or offices to maintain fiscal stability.

Including input from the project management, technical, and implementation staff often sheds new insight into which clients or client categories have the best long-term potential. This approach has the added benefit of getting everyone involved in the planning, process, and results. Having buy-in from the staff that participates in defining, establishing, and setting goals guarantees improved profitability.

COMMUNICATING STRATEGIES

Developing a strategic plan is one thing. Implementing it and keeping it viable is another thing altogether. It is difficult to pick up any modern business journal without reading about the next new thing in planning models or change initiatives.

Some believe that if you have done strategic planning, all that remains is the inspirational logo-imprinted memorabilia. You know that building and implementing a viable and dynamic plan will be challenging. It is so much more than your logo. I still have a vision-imprinted champagne bottle and a logo-inspired cloisonné lapel pin left over from failed ventures that put more emphasis on the image than substance of strategies.

The Architecture of Value

The solution, as noted before, is in keeping it simple. Trim the number of initiatives. Be less engrossed with large-scale change. Concentrate instead on small improvements. Nick Morgan, editor of the Harvard Management Communication Letter, noted, *"Above all, lose the notion that you need heroic leaders in order to have meaningful change."*[3]

Grassroots leadership is the answer: collaboration, cooperation, and individual expression based on contributions from everyone involved. This generates effective strategy more than any policy imposed by leadership or management.

STEPS TO CHANGE

In developing a viable strategic plan, there are three steps to the communication process:

- **First,** the organization's management articulates the challenges that are generating the need for change. This allows for open response, and helps establish goals. A candid analysis of the internal and external issues facing the firm, as well as obstacles to success, is essential.

- **Next,** the managing team establishes the actual change initiatives. This is where flexibility is important. Monitoring execution and adjustment to the business allow each goal to succeed.

- **Finally,** the organization reviews what worked and what failed. Accepting limitations, recognizing learning from failure, and adjusting the plan to the new realities, makes it a viable model.

Choosing not to plan strategically is not an option. Saying that you will just keep doing what you have always done fails to recognize that the world around you will continue to change in ways you cannot readily predict. Similarly, changes in your client's world offer both caution and opportunity. Be aware.

Strategy

PERSPECTIVE

I share a cautionary note. When embarking on a strategic plan, it is critical to have complete buy-in from everyone involved. Most important is the leadership of the firm. For the plans and processes to be successful, they need buy-in from everyone. Strategic efforts take time to demonstrate value.

I was part of one strategic effort that resulted in the best revenue and profit the firm had ever experienced. However, after a great first year executing the plan, the management felt they had "lost control" of the firm and returned to old policies and procedures because they had "had enough of this empowerment s**t!"

While the company's planning effort resulted in a strengthened culture and expanded sense of camaraderie, the firm's ownership could not see the value of a more flattened and more empowered organization.

By failing to follow through with the strategic planning promise for greater autonomy for each staff position, within two years there was significant personnel turnover, and a competitor acquired what remained of the firm.

IN THE NEW BUSINESS LANDSCAPE, your professional service practice will succeed when you focus on an evolutionary approach to strategic change. Evolution relies on employee self-motivation and participation, not directives from on high. It embraces change as the dynamic that keeps your practice interesting and challenging.

The Architecture of Value

CHAPTER 3 | Delivery

The successful person takes his talents and invests them in the business of living in a manner that leads to accomplishment of a full life of service.
Dr. Sol Roth

The new *virtual* practice is becoming common—one where clients, advisory consultants, implementation contractors, and even manufacturers, link together in business-to-business relationships built on mutual trust and respect. The benefits of this type of collaboration demonstrate how firms of all disciplines can leverage their expertise to deliver a completely new level of excellent experience for the client.

Defining the delivery approach your firm will take requires an understanding of the client's perspective on service value. At one time, firm leadership detested the idea of collaboration with peers or competitors—especially between marketing and business development staff. They feared leaking "secrets" that would cost them future business. Today, multi-company partnerships are common. Clients find a one-stop solution offering faster service and lower cost, and seek solutions that capitalize on rapidly developing technologies.

By collaborating with other professionals, consultants benefit from early information on upcoming product or system development. That can influence project requirements based on real-world innovation. Contractors can take advantage of the consultant's expertise and knowledge of these same developments in their analysis of the project's technical, schedule, and cost requirements.

Consultants also benefit from the practical, pragmatic, real-world field experience of the contractor. Manufacturers get critical application ideas on current product performance and new product needs. Likewise, the client benefits from receiving an improved project from this collaborative effort, as well as from being a contributor.

The Architecture of Value

Peter Senge defined the approach and processes that an enduring practice will require as the *"information age"* evolves into the *"age of integrity."*[4] Global economics puts greater emphasis on the exploration of interconnected professional relationships.

Collaboration brings new focus to the attitudinal differences between *new economy* service providers and *old school* business models:

NEW	OLD
Adding Value	Adding Volume
What Can I Give	What Can I Get
Abundance	Scarcity
Win/Win	Win/Lose
Invitation/Inclusion	Competition/Exclusion
Doing the Right Thing	Doing the Thing Right

This is a radical paradigm shift for industries marked by cutthroat competition, silo parochialism, and regional provinciality. Trust in the co-destiny of all players in the process is the important element of collaboration. From idea creation and delivery of new products and services, each collaborator surrenders some freedom and flexibility in exchange for beneficial results.

It is common for clients to support their own activities by sharing mutually critical information with the companies in their supply-chain and with their clients. As global communication networks are established, information costs become distance-independent. Relationships between traditional adversaries form to meet the clients' increasing expectations for more responsive project delivery and improved results.

Delivery

Called by various names—integrated project delivery, strategic alliance, design/build, design/assist, partnering, or advisory council—these professional interrelationships offer new opportunities to expand business. They span both technical and geographic boundaries well beyond traditional design, bid, and build structures.

INTEGRATED PROJECT DELIVERY

Integrated project delivery (IPD) is a collaborative alliance of people, systems, business structures, and practices—a process harnesses the talents and insights of all participants. It optimizes project results, increases value, reduces waste, and maximizes efficiency through all phases of implementation.[5] Created by the building industry, the IPD model can extend to any professional service that engages multiple partners in developing and executing a client's assignment.

IPD presupposes a contractual model where all parties share in the success of the project. This is a radical departure from traditional disparate client-consultant, client-contractor, and client-supplier models. IPD reinforces the collaboration model with success (and increased profitability) based on each party's contribution to the project's goals.

The adoption of IPD as a standard for collaborative practice presents challenges. As most projects involve disparate stakeholders, traditional information technology-based communication solutions are often not useful to collaboration. Proprietary firewalls, email systems, and file types can make IPD difficult to implement.

Overcoming these challenges is driving the growth of online collaboration technology. Since 2000, a new generation of technology companies evolved using "software as a service" (SaaS) to facilitate collaboration in a well-organized manner. A number of companies have developed SaaS collaboration software to automate many of the processes involved in IPD.

The Architecture of Value

Collaboration software streamlines the flow of documentation and communication and ensures everyone is working from a current version of the project. Collaboration software allows users from disparate locations to keep all communication, documents, forms, and data in one place. It assures version control with users able to view and revise files online without the need for native software. The technology also enables project confidence and mitigates risk, thanks to imbedded audit trails.

STRATEGIC ALLIANCES

In forming an alliance, firms with complementary skills agree to share resources to research, market, pursue, and contract with clients that any one of the member firms could not successfully engage on their own. This takes a commitment on the part of the leaders of each firm to use personnel and coordinate logistics to benefit the efforts of all.

Rapid and thorough communication between all participating firms is critical. By leveraging the skills of each firm, the alliance can offer clients a broader range of options, better design, and access to technology in development that might not otherwise be available. Geographical limits expand. Inherent strengths maximize.

> **PERSPECTIVE**
> The concept of strategic alliance holds great promise. There are several in the building industry (notably the *Global Design Alliance*). Having been a principal engaged in developing and supporting a multi-firm, multi-discipline, multi-geography strategic alliance, the biggest challenge came not from the top (the principals who had formed the alliance), but from the second and third tiers of virtually every member firm in the alliance.
>
> They did not understand the concept (or the value) and fought every joint project pursuit (*"Why can't we win that on our own?"*)

Delivery

> Getting buy-in from the bottom up ensures more cooperation by seeing everyone succeed.

DESIGN/BUILD

In a design/build or consult/implement project, the client enters a single contract with a single entity for all aspects of project service delivery. That contractor subcontracts all other services needed for the project. That can span concept through implementation, and can include finance and operations. Design/build can be design-led, contractor-led, or even client-led. That decision is based on which has the best capacity and greatest benefit to the project outcome.

In a traditional design/build context, the contractor responds to a basic set of criteria established by a design consultant, who may be internal (i.e., employed by the client) or external (i.e., contracted for pre-design by the client). Like IPD, there can also be the shared-risk approach where the designer and contractor team together. This can afford the client performance that is independent of specific expense demands.

The design/build team responds with design and cost proposals to meet the mutually established functional and performance criteria. Project-based teams of designers and contractors are proposed to offer clients the best of each firms' skills. This mitigates some of the challenges of traditional separate contractual relationships (and the oft-resulting litigation). This is true regardless of who takes the prime and sub-consultant roles.

DESIGN/ASSIST

Design/assist—also known as *bridging*[6]—is a variant of design/build that follows the more traditional role and responsibilities of the consultative-led design/bid/build teaming arrangement. It provides the client with early advisory services that establish performance and functional criteria, but without the same level of significant detail, or preparation of binding specifications. That responsibility falls to the contractor to implement the concept.

The advantage of design-assist to the client is the ability to tap the expertise of selected design professionals without the lengthy (and sometimes expensive) commitment to their full services. It establishes relevant criteria, and can include third-party peer review and project management oversight.

PARTNERING

Like IPD, partnering-based contractual arrangements that provide both risk and reward equally to the designer and contractor are also possible. These agreements can be an informal affiliation, or take the form of a contractual association or joint venture. From the client's view, a partners' agreement reduces the potential for change orders. It often simplifies and eliminates dispute resolution. A partnering relationship at the outset of a project ensures that the team works together for the interest of all.

Performance bonuses tied to control of cost and schedule can accelerate decision-making and true value of the professional service. One of the advantages of creating this type of a partnership between consultants and contractors is the potential for creating client loyalty that transcends the typical project relationship.

ADVISORY COUNCILS

Independent of specific projects, participation in advisory councils offers collaborative experience between technical professionals. Use councils to develop solutions to new or existing challenges. New product or service development, sales and marketing strategies, or beta-tests of new applications are all potential benefits. An advisory council provides an opportunity to engage clients in sharing thoughts and strategies that can improve your business.

Delivery

Professional societies and trade associations often provide the forums for this kind of mutual exchange of ideas and experience. Companies of all types can benefit from using outside advisory councils to evaluate and develop new markets, promotions, and distribution methods. The key to the success of these independent groups is the willingness to volunteer time and effort without the promise of significant fiscal gain. The benefit is growth of individual knowledge.

However these collaborative efforts manifest, the professional must recognize their relevance in defining service offerings. Advanced information networks fulfill the promise of instant access to communication across the globe. They can link unrelated or even competitive firms' expertise for projects. Increased communication creates the opportunity for a value-added experience for both the service provider and the client.

CHAPTER 4 | Leadership

Each one of us... must search for new and better methods—for even that which we now do well must be done better tomorrow.
James F. Bell

EVERY DISCUSSION OF WHAT IS REQUIRED for success in a professional service firm includes expertise (high levels of technical competency) and expanding the breadth of services (meeting client demand). They rarely address other important issues like continual learning, leadership development, and communication. These elements of expertise are equally important to the continued success of your professional practice.

The benefits of continual learning, improving leadership, and effective communication both within the firm and outside to your clients are critical to the continued growth of your firm, and to your personal growth as a professional.

Developing an enduring professional practice requires continuing education in the technical areas of your firm's strengths, but also in the area of personal process as well. It can set the stage for new learning and the start of an expanded career as an effective leader. If you accept the role, you will recognize the need to fulfill new responsibilities to those with whom you work.

SELF-ASSESSMENT

As you take on leadership responsibilities, you need to become more critical of your own actions, particularly when they fail to meet goals that have been mutually set with other members of your group or clients. This is a time to accept lack of knowledge or experience and to seek out new learning.

The Architecture of Value

Opportunities for the study of leadership abound; check your local colleges and universities. In addition, many of your professional associations offer courses and programs in areas of communication, team building, coaching, and practice management that can provide structure to increased learning on leadership.

For communication to be effective, it needs to have clarity. Improving interpersonal communication is the key to successful team building and teamwork. Effective communication clearly establishes common goals and interests. This is like the creation of the program statement for a building project, and equally as important to the result.

COMMUNICATION

In a design or construction practice, it is often too easy to forgo the development of the common basis of understanding and completely miss the real need, by simply trying to convince others of your ability to achieve a technically superior solution.

In my work as a technology consultant, I often found myself practicing assertive speaking as a method to reinforce the quality of my recommendations and professional credibility. This conviction comes with the inherent danger of communicating from some mistaken belief or from incomplete information. It is important to strive to improve your ability to provide educated, creative, and thoughtful input.

Providing effective feedback and balancing the needs for coaching, support, delegation, and direction with the levels and abilities of your staff are important aspects of strong leadership. The challenge remains to find new opportunities and interesting projects that will allow individuals within your firm to grow and learn.

Leaders are a combination of characteristics and behaviors. There are four notable characteristics of effective leaders. They are adept, adaptable, aligned, and agile. The behaviors of effective leaders include

Leadership

the ability to assess and to assert. They understand the value of visibility, the importance of urgency, and the primacy of precision.

CHARACTERISTICS

Adept leaders develop and apply expertise and experience to challenge. Effective leaders recognize the need to adapt and embrace both evolutionary (internal change) and revolutionary (external change) pressures on the practice. Enlightened leaders work to achieve consensus and commitment to align the firm's vision, mission, values, and culture. Agile leaders understand and change as needed to ensure the future of their practice. These leaders focus on issues of price to value, quality of service, and time to market as indicators of success.

BEHAVIORS

Successful leaders assess the state of the practice. They formulate goals that are situational depending upon whether the firm is a startup, in its adolescence, is stable and adult, or in its waning and mature years. Strong leaders need to assert. An efficient leader will initiate and be decisive, direct, and persuasive.

In addition, an effective leader is highly visible (again, both internally and externally) and optimistic. Urgency is another quality often cited in effective leaders—sensing the need to move now and quickly to capitalize on opportunity. A good leader embraces diversity, recognizing the benefit of diverse input. An effective leader is precise (i.e., communicates clearly), intuitive, and most of all, authentic.

Identifying and developing strong leadership behaviors provides the tools for responsive action. Those behaviors are the key to successfully navigating the evolutionary and revolutionary changes a professional practice faces every day.

The Architecture of Value

RESPONSE

In a professional practice, multiple projects, conflicting schedules, and personal and personnel demands become the true test for effective leaders. Lead a group in the review of conflicts to determine the real priorities. This builds teams while fostering a positive culture. Concurrently, encouraging greater communication with your client emphasizes the critical need for timely input and review on their part.

One important aspect to creating a leadership culture is developing a team charter at the first stages of project proposal planning. This is an effective method for creating greater team spirit and a sense of shared and individual responsibility to the quality of the results.

Another important element of leadership is the understanding of modes of conflict. Each of us reacts differently to difficult situations. The difference between your perceptions and those as observed by others are often surprising. As you begin to pay more attention to the styles that your associates use to deal with conflict, you can look for opportunities to foster greater collaboration.

Personality profiling, character mapping, and communications skills training can be beneficial for the personal development of both the leaders and the staff. Bringing new awareness to your personal style can create new bonds that further effective teamwork.

SYSTEMATIC LOGIC

Understanding *systems thinking*‡ is one of the key dimensions of leadership. Logic-based tools for evaluating, testing, and solving the often conflicting and chaotic problems of the day can be a great challenge. These analytical tools offer the greatest reward for leaders.

---

‡ "Systems thinking" is the process of understanding how things influence one another within a whole. In organizations, systems consist of people, structures, and processes that work together to make an organization healthy or unhealthy.

Leadership

The writings of experts on business paradigms like Peter Senge and Margaret Wheatley, among others, provide introductions and examples of systems thinking tools. They illuminate understandings of the potential for finding the core factors in the complex patterns in your organizational relationships.

Instead of challenging chaos through tighter controls, look for those methods that work within the uncertainty to create new solutions. You can often solve conflicts and foster order by being more accepting rapidly changing demands.

The emphasis on leadership puts equal importance on shared values, vision, and mission. Communication, negotiation, team building, relationships, and feedback are skills needed to practice, improve, and share with those with whom you work. Sustaining leadership and managing change are personal goals and can be the personal challenge that takes your firm to the next plateau.

The question remains: How do you develop better and more consistent self-discipline? Avoidance and denial of important, critical issues are common problems. Similarly, there is a tendency toward over-reliance on past practices and solutions that are throwbacks to old paradigms. For personal growth, focus on greater self-reflection. Seek advice and look for new opportunities for leadership learning.

AS YOU DEVELOP YOUR VISION as a leader in the application of your craft, look for methods to engender an organization that rewards individual and team efforts with equal benefits. Improving your skills in both practice and process will allow you to provide services that anticipate change and help your clients in more effective ways than were previously possible. To become a true expert practice continual and consistent learning.

The Architecture of Value

CHAPTER 5 | Style

*Leadership is practiced not so much
in words as in attitude and in actions.*
Harold S. Geneen

MANY MANAGEMENT TRENDS permeate the business environment. Total quality management, re-engineering, strategy mapping, and gap analysis define best practice methods to analyze and improve efficiencies, value, and profitability. However, no theory can successfully transform your business without the fundamental leadership that sets the context for change. Leaders create the initiatives to ensure that change occurs.

Most management experts cite leadership as the key element that differentiates the business that flourishes from those that fail. In any organization, there will be leaders, managers, and followers (staff). These roles often evolve with time and the changes in the business model and climate.

Leaders provide the vision, resources, and motivation that set the direction for the business's opportunities. The manager oversees the work. The follower does the work. A good leader develops an organization where the followers have the opportunity to grow into managers and leaders themselves.

LEADERSHIP STYLES

Leadership experts from Warren Bennis to Max DePree postulate that there are several kinds of leaders. Hundreds of companies utilize personality profiling to identify personal leadership styles. Organizational development experts study what individual styles work best with each other, and which cause conflict. Through these studies, they have identified individual styles that define effective leaders.

The Architecture of Value

To build and sustain a successful venture understand and adapt to leadership models. Four distinct archetypes[7] characterize, and resonate with inspiration:

- **The Warrior:** The leader who fits this mode is a *champion*. The warrior embodies passion for the future and fights to see that the future happens. The warrior leader has the willingness to take risks and shuns the risk averse. The warrior has the charisma necessary to rally the organization to stand up to the competition and deliver whatever it takes for success.

- **The Healer:** The healing leader is the *catalyst* for change within an organization. The healer finds and combines the different elements necessary to initiate change. The healing leader focuses on collaboration and alliances to foster change and growth. The healer seeks out the hidden strengths within the organization and combines them with internal and external resources in new ways to create methods, processes, and services. Their efforts raise the value of the company to their clients.

- **The Wizard:** The leader as a *visionary* is probably the most established model for leadership. Envisioning a larger and grander enterprise, the wizard leader has the long-view perspective necessary for success. The wizard leader integrates knowledge and learning, sees linkages, and applies that information in ways that align personal goals with long-term vision.

- **The Teacher:** The leader as *educator* is the archetype that you knew as you moved through the institutional processes of education. The teacher has the mentor's consistency and integrity needed for growth. The teacher leader is informed and aware. The teacher leader emphasizes sharing of information and applications that educate by experience.

Style

You can imagine a number of other metaphorical archetypes that may be closer to your leadership style (or those with whom you work). The military *command and control* model with its traditional hierarchies, while respected, is clearly on the wane. The *change agent* is a more contemporary paradigm. Through provocative and anarchistic transformation, the change agent can be disruptive, even as they improve the overall quality of the practice.

Self-realization of your personal style is important to becoming a leader. Focusing on developing and mastering your leadership style provides benefits to you, your reports, and your practice, and as a result, to your clients.

ELEMENTS OF LEADERSHIP

Each of these leadership archetypes has common elements used as role models and mentoring paradigms for building stronger organizations. These can help you develop your staff to take a more proactive role in organizational change.

Visionary thinking can develop alternative project and service delivery techniques, improve quality control, and create new methods for real-time sharing and collaborating. In this case, the leader's primary role is to inspire. The leader walks that important line between passion and consistency.

Strong commitment to the best interests of the enterprise and the client characterize true leaders. The leader has unquestioned integrity and is proactive and strategic. Leadership that emphasizes client-responsive behavior and efficient time management helps build an organization that provides value-added services.

Effective leaders embrace change as opportunity. The effective leader emphasizes the value of collaborative partnership and consideration of multiple viewpoints. The leader is resilient—having sustainability over time that is necessary in any venture of real worth. The leader has the

The Architecture of Value

flexibility and hardiness to survive in times when change is rapid and growth is difficult.

The leadership role is at the core of any truly valuable change initiative. Leaders provide the vision of the greater purpose, identify potential partners, organize available resources, and seek the resources needed. The leader defines the alliances between those resources.

LEADERSHIP COMMUNITY

In your organization (and in yourself), you can find models for leadership. From the CEO to the project manager, from the field supervisor to the controller, leadership is not just a position or title but the ability to create a plan and see it to fruition. It is the ability to distinguish the need to grow from the local to the global. Leaders change the focus from product to process. The leader distinguishes politics from content and is willing to learn from mistakes rather than deny them. Experimentation characterizes the best leaders.

Understanding and integrating leadership qualities is as important for you as it is for your company. It is both empowering and enabling. Leadership is about building teams that can react ad hoc and bridge cross-functional barriers. Leaders embrace technology, realizing that knowledge is the currency of today's economy. Leaders create synergy by seeing and recognizing patterns of innovation, energy, and commitment within the organization.

Developing leadership skills is an evolving process. It takes a personal awareness that recognizes the intrinsic value of the individual, the importance of the team, and the contribution of both to the larger goals of the business and your clients.

Graduate programs in leadership development are available at local colleges and universities. There are also industry-specific learning opportunities like the courses offered through many professional

Style

societies and private-sector management services. These programs can be the genesis of new awareness and skills in leadership development.

> **PERSPECTIVE**
>
> As a project manager and consultant through the first half of my career, I had very little opportunity to explore the nature of leadership, let alone think of myself a leader. Then, I received a promotion to run a branch office.
>
> I sought ways to master management skills, but that was not quite the same. I discovered the Society for Marketing Professional Services (SMPS) as a way to find new projects for my office. I got involved. I joined a committee. I chaired a committee. I ran for chapter office. I became chapter president. They saw me as a leader.
>
> From that success, I served on a national task force, which led in turn to serving on the national board of directors, and in a few years to serving as the national president.
>
> At each step in this process, I discovered that working with a group of volunteers committed to a collaborative effort for the Chapter and the Society was a great way to test and improve my leadership skills. After all, if the volunteers would follow my lead, my work should benefit from staff paid to help my business succeed. In each scenario, my confidence in my leadership abilities grew, and as a result, I achieved more leadership opportunities in my business career.

BECOMING A LEADER TRANSCENDS tactical day-to-day tasks and helps build a strategic view for both personal and professional growth. Studying, integrating, and applying the archetypes of leadership is just one method for continual learning—one that is necessary for your success. It is another step in the evolution of your expertise.

The Architecture of Value

CHAPTER 6 | People

The choice of a point of view is the initial act of a culture.
Jose Ortega y Gasset

WHETHER IT IS THE HEAT of an over-active economy or the chill of a recessive one—or something in between—the professional services industry has frequent personnel changes. People seek new positions for advancement and variety of project type. Others accept new jobs due to a soft economy or circumstances beyond their control.

What makes work a pleasure or a chore? Why do people stay? Why do they go? An enduring organization is one that values each person's unique expertise. It empowers them and provides opportunities for challenge, growth, and, along the way, some fun.

Starting a new job always comes with some level of uncertainty. Adapting to a new culture is both challenging and unsettling. It is unusual not to be frustrated. It has an impact on managers and new hires alike. The key for employees is recognizing that this is normal. The key for the employer is showing compassion. Kindness and understanding result in loyalty and friendship. Rigid behavior almost guarantees the beginnings of animosity that will be difficult to overcome in the long-term.

ADAPTABILITY

Insecurity is sometimes a good thing. If you are going to grow, every job needs to be a stretch. If you know it all, your employer may see you as unwilling to learn. Nevertheless, remember: this is *your* insecurity. A good leader provides encouragement and carefully constructed direction. Beware the superior who takes back an assignment, rather than giving you the opportunity to learn (and even fail).

The Architecture of Value

Finding challenge is an important part of maintaining a good attitude in your practice. Getting out of bed each morning and looking forward to the day is the result of a well-realized career choice. Without challenge, it is difficult to get excited about the latest new project. An effective organization works to smooth out administrative hassles. It provides tools, support, and systems necessary for productive work. As a result, it is a better place.

However, sometimes it is all right to just know your job and do it well. Lack of significant new challenges can provide the opportunity for more personal freedom in your life, and challenges of a different sort.

PLAYS WELL WITH OTHERS

Respect from and of your peers is cited as an important factor in a good job. No matter how independent, successful workers network throughout their organization. They help others get things done. As a result, they help themselves. Mentors, confidants, and trustworthy reports are the sign of a healthy company. When there is a high turnover rate, these roles are usually missing. A workplace needs to be satisfying for its people to endure.

Developing talents that are uniquely yours is an important step in work fulfillment. Knowing what makes your job best suited to your skills, or developing the skills to fit the job, can provide personal satisfaction beyond financial measure. Strive to create a company that avoids micromanagement and incompetence and empowers its people to be their best.

CHANGE HAPPENS

Career consultant and author, Dr. Carole Kanchier, stated, *"Attitudes and habits can contribute, or hinder your search for the right work."* Kanchier also comments, *"The first step is to be optimistic."*[8]

People

Developing positive, supporting, and contributing skills can go a long way to both finding and keeping a great job. A *can do* attitude and an inherent belief in yourself and those you work with are important. Rampant cynicism and negativity creates a workplace you want to avoid. A positive attitude is both healthy and contagious.

Self-confidence is another trait of leaders. This is not about bragging. Learn to self-acknowledge your achievements and document them. It helps to remember the successes when faced with a recent failure; we all have those. Building on accomplishments is easier when you have a metric from which to grow.

> **PERSPECTIVE**
> After reading about brand development in Tom Peter's seminal article in *Fast Company* magazine, *The Brand YOU!*,[9] I began to use the phrase *"blatant self-promotion"* (with tongue firmly in cheek) when it came to the use of my own of writing and speaking to express my ideas and building a personal brand.
>
> However, developing the image of the expert is more than just a public relations exercise. It means taking the risk to share your thoughts and views. I took my writing to the lectern and gave talks on the subjects for which I was most passionate. I told stories. I got more opportunities to write and speak. As a result, I gained notoriety and became established as an expert in my field.

Having the self-confidence to state a case or take a stand helps you in everyday work with both colleagues and clients. It also takes awareness that your views can be wrong or misdirected and the courage to admit your error.

The Architecture of Value

IT'S YOUR CHOICE

A good company to work for will have a clearly defined mission that states in a simple and memorable way what they do. The best companies also have a vision that states, in a motivational and affirmative way, what they aspire to be. Developing personal mission and vision statements is a positive and perhaps critical step in finding your ideal career.

Dr. Susan Harris, then senior fellow with the Advanced Management Institute for Architecture and Engineering, said in her leadership development program, *"Describing your ideal future and purpose is a good first step, but avoid having money as its sole goal. The most satisfying financial rewards come as a result of good work, not as its mission."*

Risk-taking is often its own reward. A little push often leads to great change. That can be a very satisfying experience. Understanding the sources of your fears is the first step to overcoming the barriers to change. Finding resources for support and learning can make risky change less intimidating. Living in the present, without fear of failure, is probably the biggest step to a positive future.

You know more about yourself and your career choices than anyone else does. Learning to trust your intuition—the gut answer, choice, or direction you know is right—is another major step in finding the right work in the right place. Quiet contemplation is a tool used by many to develop the meditative state that encourages improved intuitive skills.

CONTINUAL LEARNING IS A THEME I often repeat. It is a source of personal satisfaction and one that many experts in career development cite as critical to job and organizational success. Find the time, the opportunity, and support for continuing education. It provides valuable experience for both personal and professional growth, and the growth of your practice.

CHAPTER 7 | Knowledge

Unrestricted access to knowledge is what may make a vast, complex, ever changing, world of human community.
J. Robert Oppenheimer

THE PROFESSIONAL SERVICE INDUSTRY has a history of experiencing an unprecedented wave of demand followed by the seemingly unforeseen receding economy. Are there ways to predict the future reliably? Are you doing what you do in the best way possible? Is there competition you have not anticipated? Research into other business models can lead to new ways of seeing the design of your practice.

If you only rely on what you know and work within traditional delivery models (regardless of service sector), you may not see the answer before it is too late. Too often, you just do not know what you do not know. Learn from the best minds in business. Find ways to apply that learning to your business. Integrating that learning is the true definition of continual education and wisdom gained.

THE GOAL

To grow your company, it may be prudent to look outside your own peer groups and study other industries to see different perspectives. One source of new knowledge is to read the latest business press. They regularly publish concepts, anecdotes, and insights into the successes and failures of new ideas. From applied technology to futurists, there are countless good ideas. The press often shares examples of what worked and what did not.

However, it is one thing to find an example that seems to fit your view of the future, but it is another altogether to share that vision with your peers and staff. The challenge is to integrate these ideas and methods into your day-to-day operations. Then monitor and measure the viability of their results.

The Architecture of Value

Bob Prosen, consultant and author of *Kiss Theory Good Bye*, postulates that using a simple traffic signal metaphor easily conveys progress. Regularly circulating established goals accompanied by a symbolic marker in **green** ("we are on track") or **red** ("we are not," plus a definition of the appropriate action needed to improve), circumvents intra-organizational second-guessing, while strengthening a collaborative culture.

VIRTUAL TEAMS

Future forecasting can be a learned skill. It is critical to your success in the 21st century's rapidly changing economic climate. In developing your practice, take a hard look at what it will take to provide quality client service in the future.

Based on the changes that have occurred in the past few years, it seems the world is on the edge of yet another massive change. The manifestation of this transformation is the shift from reason-based to chaos-based logic. In the coming decades, three new principles will come into play:

- **First:** Reason leads to intuition. According to Regis McKenna, *"When the time between demand and fulfillment has been reduced to nanoseconds, there is literally no time for reasoned logic. Only intuitive reaction can meet the speed of the client's need."* [10]

- **Second:** The collapse of producer-controlled consumer markets.[11] In the future, the organization will evolve into a free-flowing state. With an emphasis on mass customization through one-to-one marketing, there will be a focus on the increasing customization of solutions for each client. This personalization, fueled by technology, will be the core of your business.

Knowledge

- **Third:** Global markets become irrational. The result is a splintering of social, political, and economic organizations. Ethics in this new world center on permanent flexibility, privacy, connectivity, and authenticity.

Watts Wacker shared his view of the economy in 1997, which is still applicable today:

"Houses stagnate in value while bundles of stock rise along a curve no one can understand. Instead of planned obsolescence, you have moved into an era of inherent obsolescence. The computer is outdated the moment you open up the box it has come in; the food processor breaks, you chuck it; the television breaks; out it goes... Real wealth is intangible, not tangible. The temporary is everywhere. And the temporary and intangible, lo and behold, are a perfect fit for the Age of Chaos." [12]

Wacker's long look ahead may be easy to dismiss by some as one more *new age* approach to business. However, many real-world examples and classic historical, social, and philosophical contexts establish this position as both credible and logical. Whether you have a long- or short-term personal view, there are no easy answers. Manage your way through the paradoxes and rapid changes (and the equally rapid pace of change) as best you can.

BUILT TO LAST

A more pragmatic approach in the quest for new knowledge is to look at what works for leading companies. By looking at the major processes that all businesses share and examining in detail the issues and metrics used in successful businesses today, you can learn valuable lessons.

There are many anecdotes of how new processes have helped or changed notable companies. These stories may have direct comparisons to your own operations. Focus on clients and how to

The Architecture of Value

involve them in everything from the design of services to marketing, selling, and project delivery.

There are clear definitions, methods, and techniques used in the world's best companies from cutting costs to increasing profits, all the while increasing client satisfaction. The greatest value lays in the way the theory ties to real business processes. It expands your thinking and engages you in creative problem solving.[13]

The top companies around the globe improve business performance to increase profits and you can apply these methods to your firm. They provide exceptional real-world examples of how to grow a business by focusing on client service solutions.

IT'S NOT LUCK

Tying client focus to all aspects of business process requires a thorough understanding of the personal motivations of everyone within your organization. The evolution from a traditional business practice embraces individual contribution to the collaborative benefit of your personal growth as a leader.

Developing insights into the reasons for change, methods of developing alignment, and radical (compared to your competition) transformation begins with the integration of learning from management theorists like W. Edwards Deming.[§] Robert Rodin—writing on the challenge of client service—said, *"Who in the world is figuring out how to serve clients at a lower cost? Closer to perfect for your clients' changing values? Faster?"*[14]

[§] Deming, known as the father of the Total Quality Management movement wrote nine books on the topic of business processes.

Knowledge

THERE ARE MANY PRACTICAL APPLICATIONS used for both future sight and best practice. It takes risk to anticipate and implement a new business paradigm. It takes an honest perspective to be client-focused when you cannot predict the future. How do you meet the needs of every client and still turn healthy profits? What makes the world's top companies so adept at providing stellar client service? Most important, how can you forecast and adapt your practices in a rapidly changing world?

The Architecture of Value

CHAPTER 8 | Innovation

*I became obsessed with innovation because
my clients, in effect, begged me to.*
Tom Peters

IN A CHANGING ECONOMIC CLIMATE—and one not necessarily changing in a good way—the combination of expertise and innovation is the only way to differentiate your practice in the eyes of potential clients. The professional service industry faces several challenges in developing truly innovative solutions.

On one side, you have an ever-changing and growing set of technologies with which to conceive and address new projects. On the other side, you have the tendency to fall back on solutions that have worked for many years to minimize risk and maximize profitability. However, that same safe approach means clients will also tend to shop price rather than seek innovation.

So where do you look for innovative cultures you can emulate in your company? If you have not discovered IDEO yet, you probably have not been paying attention. This creative think tank, based in Palo Alto, California, is responsible for the design of some of the most consistently influential and award-winning products, services, and now environments in the world.

THE IDEO WAY

IDEO has worked with the likes of Apple Computer, OXO, Nike, and Pepsi-Cola, and the American Red Cross, to name but a few, to develop some of their more notable products and services. For those of us working in design, IDEO brings a creative approach to its work that has implications that could benefit your own processes.

The Architecture of Value

Studying the IDEO methodology to the creative process of culture, workplace, process, and motivation may find you polishing your resume because this is clearly one fun place to work. Unfortunately, you will have to get in line because their reputation precedes them throughout the design industry, and they have many more applicants than openings.

With roots in the heart of Silicon Valley, it is easy to understand how IDEO involved many of the creative minds that brought us into the information age. Beginning with the first Apple mouse, they have continued to develop new products and services for global businesses for nearly two decades.

IDEO branched out into "environments" with interior and space design, including Amtrak's Acela high-speed train between Boston, New York, and Washington, DC. They also had a significant role in Hewlett-Packard's International Marketing Center in Cupertino, California, working with strategy/branding consultants Stone Yamashita and San Francisco-based interior architects, RMW.

IDEO bases its methodology on understanding, observation, visualization, evaluation, refinement, and implementation. Nothing too radical here—you probably think your firm already does this to some extent. However, their results are usually very cool, often amazing, occasionally disastrous (but at IDEO mistakes are "*OK!*"), and always—and I mean always—fun. Can you say that about your company's work?

IDEO bases their philosophy on the importance of innovation today. They see the value of metaphor in the mind of the client. They use time (or the lack of it) to their advantage. They explore the nature of teamwork and team dynamics. They measure the benefits of "real-world" field observation. Most importantly, they extol the advantages of freewheeling and focused brainstorming. In addition, they have a non-judgmental rapid prototyping style of project development.

Innovation

IDEO puts great emphasis on the importance and impact of the workplace environment on enhancing a creative culture.

The ten elements of the IDEO creative effort[15] are:

1. **Client Experience**: Make a great entrance
2. **Imagination**: Make metaphors
3. **Pride**: Symbols of stature
4. **Imagery**: Color inspires
5. **Clarity**: Insider knowledge
6. **Simplicity**: One click is better than two
7. **Mistake Avoidance**: Goof proof
8. **Comfort**: First, do no harm
9. **Essential Features**: Checklist of importance
10. **Options**: Offer great extras

OTHER VIEWS

Echoing the benefits of a truly innovative organization, practice strategist Ellen Flynn-Heapes, former president of consultants, SPARKS, said, *"For many firms innovation means the ability to produce new and better ways of doing things… and when driven by the firm's focus, it is the engine of wealth creation."*[16]

She went on to comment on the regimen required to be innovative. She noted, *"Perhaps the most powerful reason for focusing your expertise is to enhance the firm's ability to exchange and process information so that people can learn from experiments and mistakes, incubate and develop interesting ideas, extract problem-solution knowledge from front-line work with clients, and make better and faster decisions."*[17]

The Architecture of Value

Thought leaders approach design, operations, and marketing efforts in new, innovative, and creative ways to tell their stories and deliver real innovation. Effective service firms embrace a free-of-constraints style and develop innovative operational paradigms.

APPLYING IDEO AND SPARKS METHODOLOGIES to the relatively staid, conservative and traditional professional service processes of documentation, analysis, and management can turn the delivery of your next project into a truly collaborative and creative exercise. Assemble a cross-functional team that is motivated by the passion of the creative effort. You should aspire to this goal. The results could be nothing short of breathtaking.

CHAPTER 9 | Responsibility

Being responsible sometimes means pissing people off.
Colin Powell

IN DEVELOPING THE *DESIGN* of a professional service firm, I began by looking closely at the role the designer (the *expert*) plays in the practice. How successfully clients' expectations are met establishes brand image and reputation. Continued growth depends on how effective your design/analysis process identifies needs and translates those needs into highly functional implementations.

The elements of design fall on several shoulders during the life of a project. In the initial stages of client development, your marketing and sales staff is often in the position to hear a client's requirements. Depending on experience (theoretical, professional, and practical), the business developer may offer possible solutions or scenarios. This advice often sets the tone for the eventual design. They become critical to the process.

After the contract is established, the role of design shifts to project designers or advisors who develop the technical analysis to address the client's challenge. During implementation, a separate contractor often drives design decisions, since they are responsible for the final execution. Moreover, in many cases, these roles can overlap. Training and educating your personnel in the basic concepts of business will guide the future of your practice. They are essential to an excellent and appropriate implementation of your service.

Tom Peters said, *"Design mindfulness is the core competence... which becomes effective if (and only if) it becomes a culture of design."* [18] Developing the skills to assess client communication needs and translating those needs into a workable proposal should be the goal of all staff involved in direct client interaction.

The Architecture of Value

Does this mean everyone should be a fully knowledgeable advisor? No, but it does imply that each technically oriented person should have an appropriate level of understanding of the principles of your practice. They should understand the interaction between these processes in an integrated environment of client needs.

BASELINE EXPECTATIONS

The measure of success lies not only in meeting accepted practices and performance standards, but also in the quality, thought, and meaning that goes into your documentation. In any industry, it is important to establish, accept, and support the collective agreement for standards of performance. This allows for measurable analysis of overall performance and functionality.

Too often design criteria are ill defined. This leads to projects where success is open to question and interpretation. You will be viewed as truly valuable by your clients when you can say that the criteria for project performance has been established and documented—regardless of project delivery method—and met. Until then, you suffer the client's view that you are a purveyor of undifferentiated service.

In the early stages of a project, publish the programmatic criteria for the design. This allows the client to clarify functional needs and the designer to develop technical solutions that will meet those needs. It allows both parties to agree before the project commences. This can be as simple as a list of the functions required. For the more complex, the criterion reflects appropriately. When the basic needs are established and the measurements agreed upon, the design process can start.

QUALITY DOCUMENTATION

It is one thing to compile the list of criteria on which a design should be based and quite another to delineate a creative approach and method that will be executable in the field. The next step in design is to develop and define the impact that critical systems will have on the project

Responsibility

itself. This can include additional programmatic summaries of organizational or operational need. Technical criteria illustrate the inter-relationship between the elements of the project. It is at this stage where the creative aspects begin.

Designers or advisors then develop initial solutions through detailed planning and probable cost modeling. The work in this phase is very collaborative. It requires a close working relationship between representatives from all disciplines. Equally important is coordination with the project specialty consultants, and others who have design input (from their own perspective) for the project. This collaboration provides the necessary information to convey the project's deliverability. However, it is also the stage where the old axiom that "*a camel is a horse designed by committee*" originated. Therefore, stay focused and aware.

DEVELOPING CREATIVE SOLUTIONS that combine the capabilities of a widely disparate set of resources into a truly integrated effort is what makes being a consultant fun. Good design is not an accident or a fluke. It does not happen by chance. It is not guesswork. It is mindful and a result of the intention of expertise. The payoff of design is positive for everyone involved in the process.

The Architecture of Value

CHAPTER 10 | Consultation

I remain as convinced as ever that a high-trust method of operation is the best high-profit, high growth strategy.
David Maister

I BELIEVE THAT A COLLABORATIVE APPROACH (uniting client, designer, and implementer) is appropriate for many projects. It is superior in responsiveness and cost effectiveness to the traditional methods that have characterized the services industry for the past century. Providing appropriate counsel demands a high level of expertise. However, for a collaborative effort to be truly effective, it presupposes that the implementer has the same capabilities, expertise, and consultative-approach as the consultant.

Many contractors (i.e., anyone that implements someone else's concept) employ excellent and well-trained designers and project managers. However, when commission-driven business development professionals generate the actual need determination, the natural tendency will always be to short-circuit delivery cycles to keep the dollars flowing. While the goal of the next paycheck does not guide everyone, in a sales-motivated business model it is important.

WHO'S ON FIRST?

Many consulting professionals have degrees in their areas of expertise and certifications that demonstrate the mandatory knowledge and professional skills required for their practice. However, marketing and business development professionals rarely have the same level of training or practice metrics. This puts them at a distinct disadvantage when trying to develop appropriate scope and strategies for pursuit of large and complex projects.

The Architecture of Value

Coming from a professional service background, I am a firm believer in qualifications-based selection rather than price-driven procurement. With a clear set of requirements, interested firms can respond directly with their capabilities as they apply directly to the project needs.

Evaluating responses from qualified firms, based on a standardized set of selection criteria, allows the client, more often than not, to select the best firm for the project. Clients, who systematically collect performance data on the consulting and integration firms they use, also make better and more informed decisions.

This approach to the competitive selection process can help clients make better selection decisions. Focus on proficiency, responsiveness, cost and schedule performance, and project operational results, leads to selection based on overall satisfaction of the services received.

THE TRUSTED ADVISOR

David Maister, former Harvard University Business School professor, and renowned expert on professional practice, cites, *"The key to professional success is not just technical mastery of one's own discipline (which is, of course, essential), but also the ability to work with clients in such a way as to earn their trust and gain confidence."* [19]

Maister recommends five simple steps[20] to building trust with your clients:

- **Engage:** Use the language of interest and concern (i.e., really "care")

- **Listen:** Use language of understanding and empathy (i.e., apply your expertise to their problem)

- **Frame:** Use language of perspective and candor (i.e., relate your experience, honestly)

- **Envision:** Use the language of possibility (i.e., leverage your creativity, develop options)

Consultation

- **Commit:** Use language of joint exploration (i.e., utilize collaboration, achieve shared goals)

THROUGH THIS REVIEW, I believe that the new generation of professional service firms will focus on increasing the value of their consultative advisory services. Providing strategic knowledge to help clients plan their future—working in collaborative concert with other professionals—will supplant the traditional segregated services that have characterized the consulting industry for so long. I believe you have valuable expertise to share.

The Architecture of Value

CHAPTER 11 | Collaboration

We have met the enemy and he is us.
Walt Kelly (as Pogo)

NOTED ARCHITECT, SIR NORMAN FOSTER stated, *"I have always believed in the team approach to realizing buildings. Ideally, those concerned with construction, particularly the specialists—should be involved from the earliest stages of the project."*[21] This key factor—the early involvement of the firms with specialized expert knowledge—bodes well for the practitioners of all professional services.

A combination of knowledge, advisory skill, and technology is required for any successful consulting endeavor. It stresses the need for early input and on-going participation throughout the course of the project. It also reinforces the importance of considering alternative project delivery methods as part of your practice's long-term strategies.

Foster added, *"I believe that it is impossible to design a building without knowing how it goes together or how much it will cost. The disciplines are inseparable."*[22] Developing the business plan for your firm will require the vision for a collaborative team offers its clients excellent performance. This will require not only excellence in design, but also the follow through of quality implementation and post-implementation service and support.

A report by the University of Reading's Centre for Strategic Studies defined collaboration as *"project delivery methods that enable clients to employ one firm that takes single-point responsibility for delivering the required building and associated services in accordance with defined standards and conditions."*[23]

The study points out that these collaborative efforts provided a greater degree of certainty to clients who wanted an integrated service approach. They overcame cost and time overruns, reduced exposure to

The Architecture of Value

costly claims for change orders and additional services, and prevented possible litigation.

The market for this collaborative approach continues to grow, largely at the expense of traditional service procurement and delivery methods. Research suggests that clients and investors want projects delivered on time and budget, at the same time meeting or exceeding their need for solutions that highly satisfied those needs driving the project.

Both private- and public-sector clients are embracing at-risk collaboration as a project delivery alternative. This requires your professional service to develop an even clearer focus on meeting the needs of your clients. Leading companies will exceed expectations.

CLIENT PERCEPTIONS

As an example, the University's survey of more than 500 construction-industry clients indicated four factors and priorities for client service:

- **Delivering** higher value through better meeting the client's needs
- **Reducing** capital costs, improving quality, and lowering expenses
- **Providing** a single-point responsibility, guaranteeing a maximum price, and avoiding project-related risks
- **Receiving** greater surety of time and cost through project integration

The study went on to show that clients believe contractors add significantly to the detailed technical design process and its integration with construction. However, they do not believe they have the same understanding of process, creativity, or value. This perception, reflected in any professional service, transcends industries.

Collaboration

SCHEDULE, COST, AND QUALITY

During the same study, the University also examined more than 325 projects and confirmed the subjective belief in the value of truly collaborative efforts through objective assessment of project performance. This analysis looked at time, cost, and quality issues and the conclusions were eye opening.

They found that, on average, collaborative projects (where designer, builder, and client shared financial risks and rewards) were faster during both construction and through the total project schedule. When the contractor was involved early in the process, projects had a significantly higher on-time record. The study also showed this collaborative style reduced costs.

The conclusion would seem to be that collaborative teams provide clients with a higher degree of confidence than traditional approaches. Engage implementers early in the process and collaborative teams provide higher quality. The benefits are greatest for technically complex or challenging projects.

The collaborative approach can improve basic project delivery, reduce cost, and raise quality standards compared to conventional project implementation methods. It provides a sound basis for both mainstream and cutting-edge projects. Integrating design and implementation on a long-term basis is important to efficiencies demanded by the user.

DESIGN LEADERSHIP

When the collaborative team is design-led and guided by the need to satisfy tough, demanding clients, it succeeds at providing truly excellent service. Educating clients on the value of design-led project delivery emphasizes long-term investment in planning and defined quality. It also provides reliable information about services.

The Architecture of Value

A long-term focus is critical to building a successful client/service provider relationship. This puts responsibility on the provider to educate the client on value. Value manifests by comprehensive benchmark data. Similarly, shared investment in research focused on the client's needs yields benefits to both parties.

AN ENDURING PRACTICE

Tom Peters identified eight key elements[24] that characterize an enduring practice. In his view, successful companies in professional services develop these characteristics in their practice:

- **Flatter**: Fewer layers of organizational structure
- **Autonomous:** Be less centralized, giving more local authority to initiate new action
- **Differentiated**: Focus on value-added services in niche markets
- **Quality-focused:** Engender a consistent orientation to excellence
- **Service-focused**: Demand unfailing concentration on the client's needs
- **Responsive**: Develop a single-minded attention to timeliness
- **Faster**: Use innovation as the differentiator in your market
- **Expert:** Hire and support highly trained, flexible people

The enduring company meets clients' needs through continuous improvement and differentiated, branded projects. They provide innovation by adapting emerging technologies to their services. They educate their clients, defining best practices and performance metrics.

The enduring practice supplies *cradle-to-grave services*, and allows simple and incremental contracts that grow beyond basic scope. The next-generation practice focuses on understanding the client's perceptions of quality, design, and integrity—to build a collaborative

Collaboration

effort. They engage other trades, specialists, and suppliers. They develop integrated services that deliver style, clear choices, and value.

The enduring professional practice develops expertise in new technologies and services, and demonstrates how these relate to the clients' business. They are design-led, using skilled and experienced managers in all aspects of collaborative work. They concentrate on long-term stable markets, investing to meet client needs.

EXECUTE THESE STEPS. Listen to and celebrate your clients' perceptions. They will see the value of collaborative efforts. Deliver your expertise with an emphasis on schedule, cost, and quality and push the envelope on the application of new technologies to improve project delivery and client communication. You will have the recipe for a very successful and enduring practice.

The Architecture of Value

CHAPTER 12 | Synergy

I have yet to see any problem, however complicated, which, when looked at in the right way, did not become still more complicated.
Poul Anderson

COLLABORATIVE EFFORTS DEFINE SUCCESS. Learn to maximize the advantages of inter-organizational collaboration. Focus your culture on the benefits of those efforts. This leads to new opportunities and increased profits. Positive results come from knowledge, trust, and communication that are both synergistic and symbiotic.

Teams include many different, often complementary—sometimes competitive—disciplines necessary to conceive and implement a project. Similarly, building teams include generalist and specialty firms, as well as integrators, working together to coordinate the schedule, logistics, and implementation of the project. Manufacturers and suppliers support these efforts with product, software development and programming, and supply-chain resource and logistics management as well as through customization and adaptation.

Clients work in collaborative models as well. A client's team often includes outside members representing finance, legal, administrative, and project management. Unfortunately, while these project-focused teams often work toward a common goal, the level of collaboration is dependent on the leadership and organization defined and developed by the client, and by the ability and willingness of each single-firm member to work effectively with all of their peer organizations.

These definitions apply equally to large management advisory firms and to the smaller business of consultant, vendor, or installer. In fact, the inter-relationship of many industries reinforces the opportunity for collaboration as a means to increasing client value, and as a result, increasing revenues and profits.

The Architecture of Value

The current reticent economy market continues to challenge organizations to find new sources of revenue. To increase profitability and efficiencies, they have three options. They can buy new knowledge through mergers or acquisition. They can develop new skills internally through education and professional development. Alternatively, they can engage in inter-organizational collaboration and sharing through cooperative effort, common goals, and mutual benefits. These options apply to all areas of business, including market analysis, research and development, and service delivery.

COLLABORATIVE ADVANTAGE

For projects to be successful, clients seek to hire effective and efficient teams that understand the uses, productivity metrics, business processes, and competitive environment of their organization, and then apply their technical knowledge to the specific challenge. They count on these teams to maximize their return-on-investment for projects. This is real value, and when they are successful, everyone wins. This can be as true for a simple project as it is for a large, complex effort; it is only a matter of scale.

The key to client satisfaction with the project lies within the team's ability to:

- **Understand** and value the client's real needs
- **Address** those needs with both practical and innovative solutions
- **Implement** those results in a cost-appropriate, functional, and reliable way

However, to differentiate the service with a unique value-proposition, the ultimate solution includes something extra, something unexpected, and something beyond the basic program definition of the project.

Synergy

In order to deliver value beyond just the physical, aesthetic, or functional manifestation of the project, inter-organizational collaborative alliances approach their clients' needs with insight into new methodologies, market analysis, or image development. They support their clients by sharing valuable, unique, and difficult to imitate or substitute resources.

This approach has a competitive advantage and builds barriers-to-entry for traditional single-firm efforts. Bringing innovation and value to the marketplace is critically important to building a successful practice. It is one way collaborative efforts help all team members.

This is where a collaborative alliance has a real advantage. When design, implementation, and supply-chain work together for the benefit of the client—with the client included in the definition of the process—real productive use comes to the forefront, knowledge is gained by all, trust is built, and ongoing communication is fostered. You can apply these same efforts to improve one client's business advantage to your work with other similar clients. This increases opportunities for expanded work for the entire alliance.

KNOWLEDGE

Another benefit in bringing organizations together in a collaborative effort is the opportunity for increased knowledge. The advantages inter-organizational collaboration has over traditional project-focused teaming include:

- **Leveraging** each firm's core competencies
- **Avoiding** unnecessary duplication of efforts and costs
- **Seeing** the broader and long-term market implications of their solutions

The Architecture of Value

Applied initially to a specific project, this approach can then be adapted for other similar clients or market opportunities. Collaboration allows team members to acquire new and extensible information beyond their own resources. Leveraging this knowledge transference is dependent on alliance partner's internal approach to strategic learning and ability to apply the information to their business processes.

The success of collaborative efforts directly relates to the knowledge culture of each of the organizations involved. When companies share a strong internal focus on communicating and integrating new information, they have a better chance of successfully collaborating in an inter-organizational alliance.

A University of Ghent Leuven Management School study[25] on technological innovation and organizational collaboration defined a framework of knowledge culture that shows five levels of learning strategies that are predictive of success in building collaborative alliances. This framework is useful in the analysis of the potentials for gaining knowledge from a collaborative effort (see Figure 1).

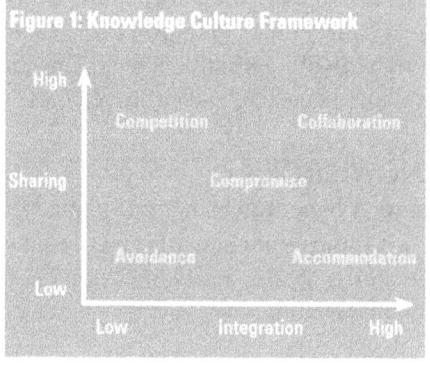

If the culture of an organization puts a low value on sharing and integrating learning, they are likely to avoid any collaborative effort. If, however, there is a greater willingness to share, but a low tendency to integrate and apply new learning, the potential exists for one firm to try to take an opportunistic competitive advantage.

Synergy

Achieving true collaboration happens when both knowledge sharing and integrating learning are common bonds between alliance members. Minimize the potential for opportunism through mutual trust within the alliance.

BUILDING TRUST

There are several factors necessary to build trust. First, the environment in which the alliance will function needs to support a collaborative approach. On one hand, if the client or market does not acknowledge or perceive an advantage, the alliance cannot succeed. However, in most cases, the bond and capacity of a collaborative alliance brings such clear benefit that this is rarely the case. A collaborative effort created without strong communication links will find it difficult to build the necessary connections for success.

Second, clearly define the tasks involved in executing the collaborative effort. Mutual responsibility is the foundation for building a continuing, trusting relationship. Next, the process used to both perform and communicate the progress and results of the effort is equally important. A common framework for both short-term and long-term efforts will avoid miscommunication and build trust.

Further, each alliance partner must bring and demonstrate the requisite skills and expertise to build the collaborative value proposition. If one partner is only present to acquire knowledge, without the ability to contribute to the common efforts, trust will be undermined. Finally, building trust takes a willingness by all parties to discuss openly individual goals and objectives and the commitment level and actions they are willing to bring to the alliance.

As with any strategic effort, inter-organizational collaboration is an evolutionary process. Built into the agreement to collaborate should be the ability to adjust the contract based on both external and internal factors. Before going to market as a team, clear expectations and motivations lead to sensible formal agreements. The quality of the

The Architecture of Value

collaborative relationship will depend on personal bonds between individuals in each organization and their trust in each other to reach their common objectives. The greater the ability to rely on trust reduces costs required by the alliance partners to negotiate and reach agreements and execute their services.

IMPROVING COMMUNICATION

Another element in effective inter-organizational collaboration is the level and quality of communication. Building processes that encourage, track, and record team interactions is critical. Proximity has traditionally been a factor in encouraging and enabling communication. However, with the increasing effectiveness of team-based collaborative tools (e.g., videoconferencing, web-conferencing, shared web-based project sites, etc.), communication and information exchange is improving. The ability to create real and productive *virtual* teams is more than ever a reality.

Successful collaborative alliances are at the forefront of leveraging the power of these technologies. They invest in the platforms and architecture of knowledge management and knowledge sharing and provide the training and incentives to see that these tools are effectively used.

INTER-ORGANIZATIONAL COLLABORATION—where disparate cultures agree to share resources and co-develop both markets and projects through formal and sometimes informal strategic alliances and joint ventures—has continued to gain popularity because it brings benefit to both the partnering businesses and their clients. Investing resources in long-term collaborative relationships can help a professional service firm expand and enhance its business while delivering new and innovative solutions its client's challenges.

PART II | **Market Your Practice**: *Sell* Excellence

In every one of us, there are two ruling principles...
one being an innate desire for pleasure...
the other, an acquired judgment that aspires after excellence.
Socrates

EXCELLENCE IS THE RESULT of applied expertise and is the message that marketing and business developers need to deliver to both existing clients and potential clients. Marketing and business development are often categorized under the term *sales* in the minds of firm principals. While related, however, they are very different and equally important. When done in concert with the firm's expertise, they are the most critical step toward success.

I think a good definition of the differences between the elements of marketing is:

> *"Marketing builds the image of the company and its brand identity, in order to **pull** clients into the firm's sphere of influence. Business development builds channels through which the company **pulls** in new business opportunities, such as strategic alliances and partnerships. Selling is all about **pushing** business into the company by pursuing specific clients and opportunities."* [26]

Marketing, business development, and sales are all related to conveying the excellence your practice can provide. This definition also includes public or media relations; a subcategory of marketing, often referred to as "communications."

The key elements of excellence are easy to identify. Mastering them is the ongoing challenge. To succeed, professional service providers articulate those strengths that set them apart from the competition.

The Architecture of Value

Time management, goal setting, accurate record keeping, and communication are important skills every firm needs. However, adding and keeping clients and increasing revenues and profits all result from successfully developing and implementing new strategies for the marketing and business development paradigm. To be a leader, you and your firm will need to develop all of these traits. Like *expertise*, there are key elements to *excellence*. Each has an impact on the effectiveness of the marketing and sales efforts of your firm.

INSIGHT

The first step to effective marketing is to develop a personal plan for excellence. Your attitude, goals, and beliefs reflect who you are to everyone you meet. Life provides opportunities for continual learning. Be a student. Success comes from being competitive, extroverted, agreeable, and self-reliant. Being defensive, uninvolved, antisocial, and bureaucratic are the characteristics that virtually ensure failure. Attitudes almost always predict performance.

DIFFERENTIATION

What is it that truly differentiates your firm from your competition? The common answers are quality, people, or service. Price is the wrong answer. Making erroneous claims or disparaging your competition is worse. To develop a competitive advantage, you have to offer your clients something unique; something that they cannot get anywhere else, something they need, and something where you excel. Educate your clients about your company's particular capabilities. Demonstrate your understanding of their problems and business issues and your experience in solving similar problems.

VALUE

An excellent way to differentiate excellence is by defining value before the sale. Provide value and you do not have to sell price. Give value and you will not have to fight price. Value provides clients with the reason

Market Your Practice

to buy. Value is the buyer's total benefit—your solution to the buyer's problems. Emphasize the features and advantages of your service to demonstrate value.

INTERACTION
Contacts, networking, and friendships will lead to more and better opportunities. Developing and implementing relational database systems (e.g., CRM) that capture the firm's knowledge and history is a key to future success. Maintain contact with clients on a regular basis, not just to see if they are buying, but also to learn what they are doing and planning. Long-term prospecting requires a philosophy of patience and sharing.

TRANSLATION
Explaining technical solutions for the non-technical client is an ongoing challenge in the marketing of your firm. Developing an understanding of the value of marketing in the hearts and minds of technical professionals is equally challenging. The two issues intertwine. Helping your technical staff learn to communicate the excellence of your solutions is critical to your marketing effort and your practice's success.

CONVERSATION
Dr. Stuart Rose pioneered a communication process called *The Mandeville Techniques*.[27] He taught that the important skill of the business developer was investigatory dialogue and conversation. Learning a client's issues provides insight into their needs. With simple, responsive and creative conversations, based around 20 key questions, you can build relationships that will provide on-going work.

ECONOMICS
Understanding the impact of economic change is critical to developing successful marketing and business development strategies. Monitoring client-side trends, learning how their business operates, and providing

The Architecture of Value

insight into potential opportunities for facilities and environmental improvements in productivity will position your firm as purveyors of excellent service.

IDENTITY

It is not whom you know but who knows you. If you are properly positioned you do not have to compete. Branding is value, image, and leadership. Competing is proposals, bids, and price wars. If you established your position as a market leader, you can win the hearts and minds of your clients. Branding requires a consistent message throughout your business. Moreover, everyone builds your brand. Public relations and marketing collateral describes who you are and encompasses what you say, how you look, and what you do.

REFERRAL

Word-of-mouth advertising is very powerful. When you finish a presentation or a phone call, leave a meeting, deliver a product, or finish a project—that is when the client starts talking. How you acted, spoke, and performed determines what they say. What they say has a strong determination on your future success. They say that performing good service may provide you with three good recommendations, but performing poorly will guarantee ten bad referrals. Which would you rather have?

NETWORK

In business development the breadth and depth of one's network defines success. Organizations that value the power of networking seek ways to engage everyone in the process. Not limited to marketing and sales staff, the most successful firms encourage everyone to be a marketer. By building a network, demand for your services will grow because the market expands exponentially with each new contact.

IMPACT

The final steps in getting a client to decide to use your service are often the proposal followed by a presentation of your expertise, your approach, and the benefits you propose to bring to the project. Developing the art of building high-impact proposals and skillfully delivered presentations can be as important as the message you have created or the service you provide.

RESULTS

The Gartner Group reported that by 2014, more than 3 billion of the world's adult population would be able to transact electronically via mobile or Internet technology. That percentage will continue to increase. Technology can provide your clients with access to your services (e-commerce), and your associates and collaborators with critical project data (intranets), and tie you and your suppliers together with key information on purchasing and logistical requirements (extranets), and testimonials of success (public relations and other social media).

FOCUSING ON THESE ELEMENTS OF EXCELLENCE does not guarantee success, but mastering marketing and business development provides a greater chance for creating an enduring practice. Businesses develop and prosper because people care about their clients, solve problems, and offer value-added services that are innovative and unique—the true result of *excellence.*

The Architecture of Value

CHAPTER 13 | Insight

You can never plan the future by the past.
Edmund Burke

EACH YEAR IT SEEMS there are many new, excellent, interesting, and insightful views for new ways of approaching the marketing activities of firms engaged in the professional service industry. Studying these ideas offers the opportunity to learn from those who stay abreast of the latest strategies and trends. Using this learning to build a tactical approach to expansion is critical to a successful marketing and business development effort.

Business legends like Tom Peters, Guy Kawasaki, and Jay Levinson have analyzed and proposed radical new approaches to practice. Each offers experience-based perspectives from outside the traditions and practices of the building industry. New thought leaders like Malcolm Gladwell, Watts Wacker, and Christopher Locke challenge traditions and conventions with knowledgeable and charismatic ideas that can be a great source of imagination and motivation to help you lead your firm to greater achievement.

Creative marketing and sales strategies often are successful when they are just that "step ahead" of your competition. As Levinson noted, "*The good guerilla fighter must out-smart and out-think the other fellow.*"[28] Keep track of those random good ideas. Memory and invention are the keys to creative effort.

TIME AND KNOWLEDGE

The effective use of time, energy, and imagination is critical. The good business developer must stay in top physical and mental shape to remain efficient. Information is a key element that will give you a leg up on the competition. Learn as much about your prospective client as you

The Architecture of Value

possibly can. If you have insights into the client's perspective of real needs, it will make the difference between you and the competition.

Surprise can be used to your advantage when other methods of introduction fail. Plan a creative way to get the attention of a potential client. Nothing (outside of bad taste) is too far out. It is often easier to reach the prospective client or decision maker early or late in the day. Important contacts are more likely to be the first to arrive and the last to leave.

QUALITY CONTACT

All employees should share proper phone etiquette and attitude. Clients turn off immediately and forever by rude manners or late (or forgotten) return calls. How your place of work is organized and maintained also sends a clear message to visiting clients. Ask yourself if your office portrays your performance.

With email, instant messaging, FTP, specialized project document sites, and overnight express delivery, there is no excuse for not getting information to them sooner than later. Keeping your firm's name in front of the client is another key element of effective marketing. Send follow-up calls, cards, or letters within two days, and continue contact one week and one month after the first meeting with a prospective buyer. Regularity and consistency keeps you "top of mind" with your potential clients.

Plan meetings with potential clients with a clear agenda and adequate time to learn everything you need to properly serve them. Do not hesitate to ask existing clients about their other projects that may need your services.

Increase your company's recognition through effective use of the media. Collaborate with your client to publish their projects. They will appreciate the opportunity for marketing themselves. Present technical papers at professional associations and become an industry expert for your local press. Participate in community service. Volunteerism offers rewards. Giving your personal time can lead to meeting like-minded peers and prospects.

IN THE PULPIT
Enthusiasm is contagious. Staff meetings, recognition systems, and promotions emphasize to all your staff that your company's service is the best. Apple Computer has an entire division (originally formed by Guy Kawasaki) called *Evangelism*, whose whole purpose is to promote the superiority of their products in every line of work. Talk to any Mac user and see if this was not an effective strategy.

From the receptionist to the field supervisor, the president to the junior engineer, positive belief in the benefits of your company's work can be the ultimate self-fulfilling prophecy. No need to denigrate the competition, emphasize the features of your solutions, the benefits of the quality only you can provide, and provide proofs in the form of examples of prior work.

FEAR THE STATUS QUO
Kawasaki's perspective includes the importance of awareness of the *sacred cow* patterns of thinking that continue to drive companies out of business. In other words, one of the most dangerous enemies of revolutionary change can be the tried and true status quo policies and practices of your own company. The best way to defeat that enemy, Kawasaki argues, is to ignore it.[29]

Kawasaki outlines several pitfalls. "The easy way (the way we have always done it) has the potential for failure."[30] On the issue of diversity, Tom Peter's is often quoted as saying, *"May the niche be with you."* However, when put to the choice, most professional service firms will opt for diversity rather than focusing on a single unique core competency or market.

The Architecture of Value

Senseless rhetoric like *"over time, any market will tend to divide into two,"* or *"diversity is a sure cure to recessionary economic times"* justifies the unachievable goal of being all things to all clients. The victims of this landmine never focus to command the marketplace. Kawasaki noted, *"The shotgun approach of going for every market at once is fraught with danger."*[31] In other words, *"less is more."*

Related to lack of focus, overextending the value and market share of an existing brand into new and untried markets is another common failing of business myopia. Recognizing the unique nature of any brand is a key to maintaining brand equity.

One of the worst practices many small successful firms make is to try to emulate large successful businesses. This may work if you really can implement their best practices, but can cause systematic failure, if you only focus on the trappings of success: opulent office space, stunning views, diversification into non-business related added "overhead."

Just to keep you on your toes, Watts Wacker postulates, *"When change is constant, it is hard to know you are constantly changing. So, too, when contradiction is constant, it's hard to know you exist in a state of constant paradox."*[32]

The challenge is to wake up to the paradoxical times you are in and adapt your personal life and your business to the unexpected. Chris Locke concurs, commenting on the impact of the Internet, *"The web has turned the world upside down and inside out. When paradox becomes paradigm, worst practices work best."*[33]

Locke suggests now is the time to adapt your services and your message to the wave of Internet-based buyers with a marketing approach that stays a step ahead of the *old guard* who are still practicing methods based on the rules in the 20th century broadcast media (and marketing) model.

Insight

WHILE MANY OF THESE STRATEGIES make common sense, most firms sabotage their potential for excellence by not using them. To be an effective marketer you have to think and work strategically and act proactively. Mastering the skills of effective marketing is the key to surviving in today's rapidly changing business climate.

The Architecture of Value

CHAPTER 14 | Differentiation

The truth is out there.
Chris Carter

THE DEFINITION OF EXCELLENCE is often a difficult one to capture. How you differentiate your firm from your competitors can be equally difficult. In the marketing effort to tell a unique story, it is often easy to slip into mythical tales of past success or a misguided metaphor for value—or worse, one of the lesser factors like hyperbolic extravagance—to describe your differences. However, the truth is often more transparent to your clients than you might otherwise think.

One of my favorite sources for practical applications for new business paradigms is *Fast Company* magazine. Their coverage is very current and hits many issues that you face in your business every day. I was particularly fond of a regular column in the early issues of the magazine, called the Consultant Debunking Unit (CDU). It looked at popular business management theories—proselytized by some of the leading consulting firms and other so-called *experts*—and tested against real-world logic.

One issue featured the popular management concept of *"picking the low hanging fruit."*[34] The theory being that when times are tough, you should market to the obvious and easy to get work. That may seem apparent, but when the CDU checked with professionals in the orchard industry, they found that this theory is more fertilizer than fact. Real-world experience shows that experienced pickers start high to carry their load back down as it increases. Further, low hanging fruit is often the last to ripen. The advice of professionals: spend the time analyzing where your best opportunities are and market strategically to what is ready. This will bring the highest value.

The Architecture of Value

Another column focused on the issue of an individual's resistance to change.[35] The *Boiling Frog* theory is a very popular consulting metaphor. It says a frog will jump quickly from a boiling pot, but when put in a pot of cold water—where the heat is gradually applied—it will stay still and cook to death. The CDU found that in reality a frog would jump from any pot, hot or cold (or getting warmer). The conclusion: Change is random more often than it is predictable. The recommendation: provide a satisfying environment for your people, or they are likely to jump.

I continually find similar myths in selling strategies of the building industry. The perspectives of the design consultant and the contractor are often at odds. Worse, what is often purported as truth during the pursuit of new project opportunities often stretches the limits of credulity. Unfortunately, the stories told to the uninitiated (often the end-user client) often sound good in theory, but hold little water when put to the test. Some examples follow.

INDEPENDENCE AND BIAS

Consultants often say they are without loyalty to any one particular brand or product line. This allows them to choose the best products for price and performance for a specific need. In reality, both consultant and contractor have biases. Some consultants base their views on experience; what has worked in the past—is safe. Some base them on theory; what the manufacturer says it will do looks good on paper. Some are based on whim; *"I've always wanted to try that, and, hey, it's somebody else's money."* Some views are based on recent awareness; which manufacturer or sales rep just presented their latest product, fabric, finish, gizmo, etc., with lunch (or dinner) included.

Differentiation

PERSPECTIVE
On the subject of food, I have observed within many segments of the service industry that—rather than the inherent quality of their products—certain components are often selected based on the manufacturer or their representative wining and dining key consulting staff to gain mind share. One brought in a tray of their mother's recipe for homemade lasagna to feed our office. Then their competitor took us out for a dinner of fine French cooking and a vintage (and very expensive) Chardonnay. Product representatives use this process across almost all disciplines. It is unfortunate that *top of mind* is sometimes only a result of *full of stomach*.

The counter view would say that the contractor with real world experience—based on having to build, test, and support after the fact—provides the client with recommendations based on what will perform the best for the given functional need. I know of very few contractors that stock all (if any) of the materials needed for a simple or complex project.

SAVING THE CLIENT MONEY
Who does that best, consultant or supplier? That depends. If the consultant's design includes fully coordinated plans, and all related infrastructure, schematics, and list of components, the result can be a truly apples-to-apples bid.

The competitive marketplace (and any contractor's willingness to shave margin) will probably provide the lower cost solution, but at what other hidden cost? The consultant still has to account for the time to develop the design, coordinate the plans, issue the documents, and provide the implementation phase follow-up. When all you sell is your time, you had better have a healthy margin on the cost of your time or you *will* lose money.

The Architecture of Value

In reality, most consultant specifications lack required (or desired) detail, not because of blatant omission, but simply due to the economics of the business. Clients are rarely willing to spend the money for the time necessary to completely design and engineer a project and coordinate the associated implementation.

Thus, you see varying degrees of performance specification masquerading as an engineered specification *("and now magic happens")*. Therefore, a designer/builder collaborative approach that includes all of the above (*"it's necessary to get the system to work anyway"*) will usually have the lowest bottom line cost.

KNOWLEDGE

Contractors who rely on bid opportunities do little to counter the argument that the all-knowing, responsible, and educated consultant is king (or worse, priest), lest they anger the source of potential ongoing business. In reality, the training and experience of the project engineers and managers (and many account reps) in most contracting firms is, more often than not, better, more germane to real-world issues, and more complete. As to responsiveness, that is an individual issue. I have known responsive and unresponsive (*how soon do you return calls?*) on all parts of the services industry.

Business relationships succeed only when there is mutual respect between all parties—the client, designer, and implementer. One position of the design/build faction of business is that, under the roof of the integrated contractor, the two efforts work in concert. The best in the professional service industry are allies who combine resources for collaborative and profitable work. It is important to understand each of their perspectives—and yours.

Differentiation

There is an old saying that purports:

"Architects are generalists who go to school to learn a little about a lot. Then they go through their careers learning less and less about more and more until they know nothing about everything.

On the other hand, engineers are specialists who go to school to learn a lot about a little. Then they go through their careers learning more and more about less and less until they know everything about nothing.

Unfortunately, contractors, who are often very wise and know a lot about everything, end up seeming to know nothing about anything—mostly due to their association with architects and engineers."

Compound that bit of wisdom with another old adage that, *"Those who can, do, and those who can't, teach—and, those who can't teach, consult!"* Now you have the potential for real conflict. Trained as an architect, practiced as an engineer and consultant, and having helped lead a major contracting firm, I cannot really debunk these theories.

LEST YOU THINK this a thinly disguised plug for contractors at the expense of designers and consultants, I could have just as easily redirected this chapter to the opposite view in Chapter 9. Neither perspective is without its questionable practices. My hope is that in your marketing efforts you avoid the traps of unfounded myths, misplaced metaphors, and rampant hyperbole. Instead, focus on ways to define excellence for the client's benefit and honestly demystify your role in the process for the betterment of the industry as a whole.

The Architecture of Value

CHAPTER 15 | Value

They are only great who are truly good.
George Chapman

PROVIDING VALUE HAS BECOME the definition of excellence and the key to successful growth in the building industry. Can you continue to work in the same way you always have? Probably not, if you are to succeed—let alone survive. Your clients are demanding value through more flexible and broader services.

As the global economic engine drives inexorably forward, it may seem to offer less opportunity for innovation and creativity by the practitioners of professional services. This does not necessarily reflect a loss of vision. More likely, it is the response to the client's demands for more comprehensive service that reflects the importance of time-to-market (faster), quality performance (better), and cost-to-value to the client's business (maybe, maybe not, cheaper).

How can you bridge the gap between "*how it is always done*" and "*how it must be done*" today? The first step is to describe the value of your traditional services in new (the clients') terms. It is important to develop client relationships that allow for open and honest assessment of need and provide avenues for research into operational and functional requirements.

Address complex issues of maintenance and cost to provide cost effective and efficient solutions. Clients will value creativity delivered in a form that gives them a competitive edge and provides flexibility to accommodate change.

One of the ingredients of a successful project is a design team made up of representatives of the client, designers, and contractors who are willing to work together toward a common goal. Conflicting issues need

The Architecture of Value

to be resolved early to prevent adversarial attitudes from developing. Everyone benefits from mutually understood project goals.

An initial *kick-off* meeting to review important planning and logistic issues with all participants is a very common method. A more radical approach that engages all parties in a thorough overview of goals, and includes teambuilding exercises, may have better long-term results. In a focused teaming session, it is important to not only include senior representation from the client, but also representatives from all of the primary teams, as well as the specialty consultants and contractors that will have input during the project.

This is the true meaning of collaboration. A facilitated partnering session (by someone outside the project team and independent of a personal agenda) can bring out all of the critical logistics and inter-related activities that will make the project a success. Leaving out anyone or minimizing their ability to see and understand the *big picture* will be the cause of potential problems in the end.

PERSPECTIVE

I have been involved in many projects where key client stakeholders or inter-related design team members were not available or accessible—kept at "arm's length" by a project manager or third-party owner's representative. The result was less without it and usually a mess because of it.

Conversely, when everyone is in the communication loop, projects tended to go more smoothly, and in the end, satisfy both the client and the design team. Communication improves when the client is actively involved. When they are not, it becomes more critical to take a proactive role in maintaining a high level of information exchange.

Value

In dealing with other professionals on the project team, mutual respect between each discipline is important. When technical and design competence is acknowledged, real issues can be openly discussed.

SHRINKING SCHEDULES

Project schedules are compressing. Every week you see new projects being requested that have shorter and shorter timelines for completion that are reflective of the client's own competitive marketplace. The ability to deliver design and documentation rapidly is critical to meeting the client's need.

Clients continually cite *communication* and *responsiveness* as the key skills that differentiate their suppliers (of both goods and services). While fast track projects may afford the client savings, they are rarely without a significant impact on the designers and contractors involved in the project. More reason for communication.

INNOVATION

What are new services you can provide? Instead of being reactive or better, proactive, author Daniel Burrus suggests that you become *"preactive."*[36] Study your client's business and business processes. Seek opportunities that help them improve. Look for solutions to problems your clients do not realize they have. Just providing technically appropriate solutions is no longer acceptable. You must understand broader issues and provide results that improve productivity.

Burrus uses the AT&T television commercials of the mid-'90s (*"Have you ever... no, but you will."*—implying that AT&T will provide it) as a good example of presetting the minds of potential clients with the ability to provide innovative solutions.

One area gaining popularity is outsourcing. With flattened organizations, augmentation by outside contract employees has become a profitable way to provide *just in time* service.[37] Many

The Architecture of Value

opportunities exist to provide management and support personnel to supplement the client's employee base as they downsize and focus on their own core competencies.

THE VALUE PROPOSITION

In the face of a price sensitive, economically driven project selection process, how do you secure new work? Convey value. In responding to the next request for proposal, first identify and state your client's real concerns. Then describe your approach to these concerns. Finally, provide examples of similar solutions for similar problems. Anecdotal stories are a powerful medium to illustrate your technical excellence (e.g., *"This is how the performance of our design reduced the cost of this client's operations."*)

In my own practice, we were very successful by demonstrating a well-defined process, illustrated by photos of real (and similar work) and samples of all phases of project documentation, that clearly show the client the *"who, what, how, when, and why"* of our approach. Many times this resulted in contracts where the fee was significantly higher than that of our competitor, but where our direct benefit to the project was much clearer in their minds.

How do you know if your previous solutions have been notably successful? Ask questions of past clients. Too often, you finish a project and simply go on to the next without ever looking back. Take time to conduct post-occupancy valuation studies. Establish a communication process at the beginning of the project that will pre-set the client for ongoing review of the progress of your work in their eyes. This client relations work can focus future efforts on both those areas where you excel and those where you are perceived as being deficient.

How do you position your firm as innovative? You must find and show the essential difference between your work and that of your competition. It is probably not just better documentation. Most firms have powerful computer-aided-design systems. They use desktop

Value

publishing and database systems. It is important to express benefits and proofs, not just competent service. This requires an investment in training, technology, creativity, and a willingness to change. In areas where you are weak, strategic alliances can build relationships that offer both parties the opportunity to learn and grow.

WITH FEES MORE COMPETITIVE, schedules more demanding, and projects requiring more and more specialization, the future holds challenges unlike any you have faced in the past. Demonstrating and providing value will be the element that defines excellence and differentiates your firm from your competition. Value will assure your place in the professional service marketplace.

The Architecture of Value

CHAPTER 16 | Interaction

You cannot improve interdependent systems and processes until you progressively perfect interdependent, interpersonal relationships.
Stephen Covey

SELLING EXCELLENCE is often a function of knowing what went right (or wrong) in the past. One of the topics that firms continue to explore is client relationship management (CRM). There are many programs that help collect, categorize, and collate the rich (and valuable) knowledge history of your organization.

However, CRM is not just software and technology. Engraining CRM in the processes of your practice is the only way for it to be effective. CRM is all about developing a strategic framework for knowledge management and implementing the processes to match your business needs to your client's requirements. Look at CRM technologies by asking what they can do from the business perspective.

Every firm goes through three distinct phases with its clients—acquisition, retention, and enhancement. It is important to define CRM goals for each phase. Clarifying your current strategies and practices is critical before undertaking any CRM solution. The goal of an effective CRM system is to organize your internal knowledge history in ways that maximize client value through simplified, customized engagement and transactional processes.

The right CRM solution increases profitability by clarifying and defining the effort required to match the client's expectations. When implemented successfully, a CRM system makes your company client-centric, putting your client's needs first in the minds of everyone in your organization.

The Architecture of Value

To be effective, a CRM solution needs to engage the client in ways that simplifies their interaction with your company, speeds delivery of your services, and, ideally, saves them money, while increasing your profitability. At the same time the CRM system collects, categorizes, and sorts information that will allow you to provide increasing value-added services to the same client, and attract new clients as well.

WHY CRM?

The business processes of the typical professional services firm interact with the client at many different points. They include:

- **Front-end** contacts of marketing and business development (acquisition)

- **Mid-cycle** contracted services of consulting, implementation, and service and ongoing back-office services of purchasing, billing, and collections (retention)

- **Back-end** creation of customized services specific to each client's needs and preferences (enhancement)

CRM allows you to document and mine data for trends, hiccups, and successes based on the client's experience. Consolidating, categorizing, and analyzing that information and experience can provide invaluable data that allows your company to better serve with services that anticipate their buying patterns, lower their budgets, exceed their expectations, and improve their scheduling requirements.

Robert Rodin said the ultimate client goal is moving quickly from cheaper, better, or faster toward *"free, perfect, and now."*[38] However your clients view service, it is time to look for innovative ways to maximize delivery value, improve service quality, and minimize costs through well-defined and practiced processes.

Interaction

Industry surveys consistently show that CRM installations fail to meet all goals. They are often late and over budget. Many do not produce meaningful results.[39] Recent surveys show the failure number reduced, but concerns remain. This indicates that vendors and clients are taking more time in developing and implementing systems.[40] However, these are not positive indicators. However, CRM can be successful.

As companies integrate their marketing, project management, and financial systems into common technology platforms, it becomes easier to expand these systems to include input and response from clients and alliance partners, as well as the staff.

THE CURRENT LANDSCAPE

Through the '80s and '90s, simple personal information management (PIM) software provided a convenient way to replace the business card rolodex and add notes, documents, and histories to individual contacts. The personal digital assistant (PDA) made this information portable.

Today, products like Microsoft Outlook™ fill that same niche on virtually every desktop, laptop, and smart phone. However, they only begin to connect with the total of all client interactions that further the mutual, and hopefully, growing relationship between your company and its clients.

There are many solutions for large-scale, multi-national organizations and more scalable and cost-effective systems for mid-size and smaller firms. Application service provider (ASP) solutions serve multi-office or geographically disperse teams using a SaaS approach. A central server hosts these solutions.

The Architecture of Value

This allows your staff to access data via a web-based interface from virtually any location. Many companies are developing *cloud-based*** comprehensive tools for engaging, gathering, organizing, and sorting myriad data types and information that are relevant to each client.

The evolution of the Internet has provided interesting solutions for client interaction, beginning with the basic website *brochure*. Intranets allow for internal information and best practice sharing. Extranets allow the client to input, access, and modify selected information (e.g., FTP drawing and document sites).

The newer cloud-based systems offer many of the features of the traditional PIM (i.e., contact information and histories), and add document posting/sharing, e-commerce, and threaded discussion groups. They are accessible from anywhere your staff, supply-chain partners, or clients can connect to the Internet.

However, web and Internet technologies are only delivery and integration mechanisms. Most clients still interact with their advisory consultants through traditional channels. They post a request for proposals (RFP) or qualifications (RFQ), and follow-up by scheduling live presentations (acquisition).

The reports, specifications, and drawings you create define the route to the completed project (retention). Post-project warranty monitoring services define the support needed for ongoing additions and changes to the implementation (enhancement).

Base your choice of CRM technologies on improving client acquisition, retention, and enhancement through any channel, not on whether your client base uses the Internet.

** Cloud computing is location-independent computing, whereby shared servers provide resources, software, and data to computers and other devices on demand, as with the electricity grid.

Interaction

THE NEXT WAVE

Developing an overriding knowledge-based, client-centric culture is the goal of the ultimate CRM solution. Getting there requires the same discipline for strategic planning, practice, and process execution that characterizes the best-of-class companies throughout the business world.

The strategic development process necessitates a shared business vision (what your company aspires to) and mission (what your company does every day to achieve that vision), an understanding of the competitive landscape, knowledge of market opportunities, and a long-range view of potential change in the client base and buying characteristics.

Targeting specific granular segments of clients requiring the services of your core competencies is an excellent way to start an effective CRM process and begin to define true value creation in the eyes of the client.

The value-creation proposition is at the core of an effective CRM system. What value does the client receive (and more importantly, perceive) from your service? Is value *objective* (dollars per square foot, improved productivity, etc.) or *subjective* (improved morale, communication, or identity)? Your client will tell you, *if you ask*.

Equally important in the assessment of value your organization receives from the relationship with each client. Evaluating the acquisition economics (*What did it cost to get this project?*) and retention economics (*What did it cost to keep this client?*) are necessary to focus on those clients who provide profitable work, and to avoid those that do not.

Integrating all of the physical (business development, direct marketing, phoning, office visits, project management, project documentation, project execution) and virtual (email, website, intranet, extranet, e-commerce) client touch-points in a way that seamlessly collects and

The Architecture of Value

retrieves information from a common data repository is the key to the CRM solution, and its greatest challenge.

It takes a mutual understanding (vocabulary) and desire (practice) at all levels of the organization. CRM combines an investment in information technology systems, analysis tools, and integrated front office and back office applications, to make it all work together. The work to develop a CRM system is daunting, but not impossible. It will be time consuming, but mission critical. Relational enterprise processes are the foundation of the client-focused practice. A comprehensive, knowledge-management environment will be required if your organization is to survive in the 21st century.

At the end of the day, performance assessment will tell. The CRM system can be considered a success, if shareholder value is improved because of employee value (individual performance and productivity), client value (more profitable work because of retention and enhancement), and cost reductions (a drop in overhead costs). Effective performance monitoring requires established (and communicated) standards, metrics, and key performance indicators (goals) be understood by everyone in the organization.

BECOMING CLIENT-CENTRIC

Organizational change that emphasizes and values business intelligence and knowledge management requires a linkage between leadership and management behavior. A CRM solution can only succeed when the firm's hierarchy fully supports the initiative by reinforcing employee attitudes that recognize client significance, importance, and consistent client satisfaction. The results are increased revenues and, profits, and, therefore, shareholder value.

There is a vast array of potential CRM options—from contact management to e-procurement, from customized project configuration to alliance partner management. Developing an effective strategy and

Interaction

performance metrics, based on just a few functions, will increase your chances of enjoying a successful CRM implementation.

ONCE RESULTS ARE CLEAR AND VALIDATED, expand your CRM system to encompass more of the organization's client-focused processes. However, be cognizant that the amount of change needed to implement CRM technology increases dramatically with the number of desired functions. In the end, the increased access to truly valuable knowledge is worth the effort.

The Architecture of Value

CHAPTER 17 | Translation

*There are two ways of spreading light;
to be the candle or the mirror reflecting it.*
Edith Wharton

AN IMPORTANT CONSEQUENCE of the technical professional's position in your practice is that, because of their specialized expertise, they need to be able to describe technical solutions to a broader, more generalist audience—your clients and potential clients. This ability to create a common vocabulary and depict sometimes-complex capabilities and functional inter-relationships in both written and diagrammatic form is critical to defining the benefits of your service.

While it is probably not realistic to expect every technical specialist to be capable in all aspects of the competencies necessary to define, train, manage, and develop your business, it is critical that there be efforts to educate them well enough to communicate the essence of the solutions you espouse.

As a principal of a design consultancy, I became increasingly concerned about the compartmentalization of knowledge and its effect on our competitive standing in the building industry. This *silo* mentality was frightening in its implications. As an observer of professional practices, I noted that what happens on a local and personal level is usually reflective of broader issues having an impact on companies throughout the industry.

INVOLVEMENT

I have come to believe that, in the end, you will pay the price for principals, staff, and project managers who distance themselves from clients and resist learning key disciplines—one of the most important being marketing. By marketing, I do not just mean promotion, communication, or sales. For the professional, being able to market

The Architecture of Value

their ability to describe and explain your services in a clear and concise way conveys meaningful and competitive value to the marketplace.

Increasingly professional services firms are failing to live up to their promise of improved productivity and profitability for the business, service, and manufacturing industries where they are hired. That failure results largely from the disconnection between practice and marketing. The problem is not the practice itself, but the gulf between the delivery of quality solutions and the means for users to understand the benefits they receive from them.

CONSULTATIVE SELLING

Integrating marketing and technical education is not a popular concept among designers, engineers, or project managers; nor is the discipline necessary to define technical concepts popular with dedicated sales and marketing professionals.

It is necessary for both sides of the profession to improve as you adapt new project delivery systems with increasingly complex components, integration, and logistics. Marketing is one of the cornerstones of effective technical services learning, which integrates interpersonal communication, ethics, and teamwork skills.

As we emerge into the *new normal* economy, technological developments will be major drivers of organizational change. Mass-customized designs will replace the standardized approaches of the past. The professional service practice needs an increasingly trainable workforce, not just one that is highly trained. Leading organizations will be *learning organizations* where everyone identifies challenges and develops solutions through teamwork and cross-functionality.

Warren Bennis noted, *"Leaders are not made by corporate courses, any more than they are made by their college courses, but by experience."*[41] He observed that an organization's commitment to provide opportunities to staff, through experience, allows for both growth and

Translation

change. When your technical staff can share that experience and the applications of technology that they have discovered with their clients, they will have found an invaluable resource to the firm and themselves.

Peter Senge commented, *"Over and above self-interest, people truly want to be part of something larger than themselves."*[42] Finding ways to develop a *shared vision*, which combines both your corporate mission and the client's vision, leads to successful projects.

Radical measures may be required to get you closer to this kind of integration of knowledge and flexibility of mind that the business world demands. To broaden knowledge, your business needs to develop internal training and education systems that link the interrelationships between the science of your practice and the practice of your science. The quality of written and oral communication is as important as an engineer's knowledge of a technical subject.

This is more than just being proficient as technical writers and analytical readers. Professionals who can communicate clearly and concisely, regardless of medium, with appropriate information within the context of their profession, will be the ones who are in demand in the future.

TRAINING IS KEY

Teach the value and methods of effective teamwork. One of the benefits of internal team efforts is an improved approach to participating in larger project teams that span multiple participants and companies. Again, communication is critical.

Emphasizing the importance of integrating marketing—particularly public relations, awareness, and communication—with the skills of technical engineering is important to your success. Any solution must come with the means for the larger client community to see its benefit and application.

The Architecture of Value

Successful companies require designers, engineers and project managers who are comfortable with the idea that marketing to define the service and determine the client's needs and requirements. Immersed in your own area of practice, you may often forget that you still need to *sell* your innovative solutions.

MASTERING PROFESSIONAL SERVICE MARKETING is important as we move closer and closer to a knowledge economy. Business leaders should think hard about their hiring strategies. Look beyond just hiring professionals with the right skills to hiring people with the right talent—the talent to learn new skills, perform multiple roles, and understand the needs of the total organization. With these skills in place, you effectively practice your role as translators of solutions.

CHAPTER 18 | Conversation

Judge a man by his questions, not by his answers.
Voltaire

IN THE PROCESS OF BUSINESS DEVELOPMENT, you identify, research, and meet with potential clients with whom you want to work. By learning about their needs and goals, you are able to develop and present solutions that generate projects for your firm. Even if they do not have immediate needs, building the relationship can lead to opportunities later on.

However, too often, marketing and sales representatives spend too much time talking about their company and its history (bad) or themselves and their personal experience (worse). They put emphasis on *"who we are"* and *"what we do"* and, especially on *"why we are great,"* and end up *we-weing* all over the potential client. One client described it as, *"They show up, and throw up!"*

Marketing is all about message. Business development is all about relationships. Sales are all about meeting a specific need. If your marketing effort has provided a consistent message that communicates the value of your service, you may get the opportunity to build the relationship in the business development stage. Without the relationship, you will never get to the sale.

The initial dialogue with a potential client is a method to gather diagnostic information. It provides opportunity for analysis and synthesis of key insights into their needs, fears, experience, and goals. The focus of this first encounter is the non-physical goals (why and why not) that the results of any project need to accomplish. Use the discussion to identify their concerns, feelings, and priorities.

There are three simple elements to a successful client development meeting. First, control the energy of the meeting. Let the client talk; you will get your chance later. Next, be comfortable. Set the meeting

The Architecture of Value

environment for your comfort, not theirs. This will allow you to stay in the moment. Finally, establish authority. Be firm and strong, take charge (but be professional). Being self-assured sets you apart as the *expert* in their mind.

There is a simple process to a successful dialogue. Based on Dr. Stuart Rose's *The Mandeville Technique*,[43] it includes 20 basic questions. There can be more, but rarely less. It is important to stay in sequence. This will lead the client to sharing important information and position you for a successful response.

Before you begin, state the agenda. Begin the meeting, saying, *"I'd like to take a few minutes to find out about your company* (or project) *and any of your concerns* (about working with service providers), *and then answer any questions you may have about our firm."*

Most meetings start with the normal kind of ice breaking; small talk about the weather or current events. That is fine. Let the conversation follow your style, but always be aware of theirs. Do not try to be what you are not. As noted before, do not self-aggrandize. There is nothing more off-putting in the initial phase of building a client relationship than egocentric diatribe. Use a notepad. Take copious notes. It shows interest and gives you key points to follow-up with later.

DETERMINE GOALS
In the first step, determine their basic needs, objectives and concerns.

1. *What generates a need for a consultative project?*
2. *What concerns or goals do you have for the result?*
3. *What kind of help do you need?*

Use open-ended questions (*who, what, where, why,* and *how*); avoid questions that can be answered yes or no. Listen for any words that imply ambiguity for their needs, investment, or image. Explore service delivery options.

Conversation

Summarize by saying, *"I understand your goals are...; your concerns are...; and, your objectives are..."* This active listening technique helps the client know you are listening and understand their concerns.

GATHER NAMES

Again, using open-ended questions, explore key decision makers and outside influences that may be important in securing the approval for the project.

4. **Whose ideas generate projects?**
5. **Who supports these projects?**
6. **Who usually opposes them?**
7. **What is the source of funding?**
8. **Who is already working on similar projects?**

Again, summarize by saying, *"I understand your projects start as...; the support comes from...; the opposition comes from...; the budget comes from...,"* etc.

THEIR INVOLVEMENT

Learn about their role and their perspective on the project through a series of questions that will help determine decision priorities.

9. **How do you get involved in projects?**
10. **How do you feel about your role?**
11. **Have you had projects that were successful? Why?**
12. **What is your role now? What will it be in the future?**
13. **Who decides who manages which project?**
14. **How decisions made?**

The Architecture of Value

Again, summarize. It is important to maintain the *active listening* role, both for their comfort and confidence in you, and for your need to ensure that you have heard their concerns correctly.

WHAT THEY EXPECT FROM YOU
The next series of questions helps to identify their view and understanding of your professional service area and scope.

15. *How do you feel about other firms you have worked with? (Do not point fingers!)*
16. *What kind of firm do you have in mind for your projects?*
17. *What criteria do you use to decide on the firm for a project?*
18. *What preferences do you have for fee structure?*
19. *What is the period for solicitation and award of a contract?*
20. *How are projects funded?*

Again, summarize.

PROMISE A RESPONSE
Conclude the analysis phase of the meeting with an acknowledgement of their contribution. *"Thank you for your time. I want to take this information back to our office. Let me bring back a summary of your goals and concerns as we discussed, and our initial ideas for an approach to meet your project needs."* This sets the stage for on-going dialogue. Set a date for your response, and schedule a follow-up meeting at this time. A good rule for all client interaction is to *"book a meeting from a meeting,"* ensuring that you have set an appointment to see them again.

Conversation

OPEN THE DIALOGUE

At this point, it is appropriate to turn the table and answer questions about your firm's capabilities. *"What questions can I answer that you may have about our firm or our experience?"* Answer only facts. Do not offer answers to any questions that require judgment. Defer to the team for review of issues. If their time is short (less than 45 minute, typically), set another meeting to answer other questions and to meet other members of your firm.

GETTING REAL

As part of the strategy of developing your practice, it is critical to know what projects to pursue. Equally important is which projects will be profitable. The key to that understanding are your initial conversations with the potential client.

Selling is the second oldest profession, and often confused with the first. For many in professional services the "S" word carries so much baggage that it is called "business development." Customers are afraid that they will be "sold" a bill of goods and sales people fear they will not make the sale. In the quest to close the deal, they too often lose sight of the real grail: understanding and satisfying their real needs.

In his book *Let's Get Real, or Let's Not Play*, Mahan Khalsa, a sales expert in the Franklin Covey organization, defines why helping clients succeed is essential to the success of any business.[44] His process sets up the agenda for effective dialogue that almost guarantees productive communication. By focusing on key areas of customer insight, you can use to determine what their key issues are, and whether or not you can help them find a solution. His program follows these four questions:

1. **Problem Evidence:** "How specifically does this problem manifest?" How do you know it is a problem? Too much, too little, or what?

The Architecture of Value

2. **Problem Impact:** "How big?" In dollars or on a scale of 1 to 10? Implications? Worst-case scenario?

3. **Results Evidence:** "Measure of success?" Increase, decrease, or what?

4. **Results Impact:** "ROI?" Direct? Opportunity? In dollars or on a scale of 1 to 10? Implication? Best-case scenario?

TO GO OR NOT TO GO?

When times are good, it is easy to be selective about which projects to pursue. When the economy is sluggish, it is equally easy to chase "anything that moves" because of fear that there will not be enough work. In either scenario, an effective "Go/No-Go" decision process can help you focus on the work you can win, as opposed to the work you can chase.

I believe there are ten simple factors that when reviewed at the outset of identifying any project opportunity can make a difference in not only winning, but in not spending time, effort, or dollars that could be better spent to improve the relationship with a target client.

GO/NO-GO CHECKLIST (Saying "Yes" to 50+ percent is a "Go!")

1. **We know someone** (a decision maker in their company who likes us)

2. **We know someone** (an influencer who they trust)

3. **We have a reference** (a champion from outside their organization who will recommend us)

4. **We have worked with them before** (and it was successful)

5. **We have done projects "just" like this** (for them; they were successful)

6. **We have done projects "just" like this** (for someone else, and they will give a good reference)

Conversation

7. **We knew about the project "early"** (i.e., +90-180 days before the RFP/Q)
8. **We can make money** (profit)
9. **We have available resources** (an "A" team who can lead the effort)
10. **We have a "win" strategy** (that leads to a beneficial solution for the client and a differentiator against the competition)

If you use this type of qualification process, you will win more and develop stronger relationships. It will focus your efforts and enable you to develop stronger "trusted advisor" relationships that are a based less on selling, and more on your expertise.

THESE TECHNIQUES WILL HELP you focus on developing client-centric dialogue. It focuses the energy on their issues and allows you to position your response to meet their specific goals and objectives. It provides the information you need to answer their questions. With responsive and creative solutions, you build relationships that will continue to provide on-going work and referrals.

The Architecture of Value

CHAPTER 19 | Economics

In economics, hope and faith coexist with great scientific pretension and also a deep desire for respectability.
John Kenneth Galbraith

AS WE MOVE PAST the first decade of the new millennium, there has been plenty of talk about the unstable economic climate. To avoid a recessionary impact on your business requires applying on-going strategies. Whether you believe you will survive through a *soft landing*, or suffer through a significant downturn in growth, there are steps you can take to protect your business from an uncertain future.

The first step in a down time is to look hard at the business of your business. Strategic planning should be a regular exercise shared by management and staff. Continual review of your core values and aspirations can help your company stay focused. Understanding how your firm approaches development goals relative to growth and diversification will determine direction.[44]

Are your financial goals consistent with your markets? What key financial indicators do you monitor and with what regularity? Does your current business mix support your goals? Are your business developers working in concert with the company's vision? An important indicator is the satisfaction that your staff has with their work and their workplace.[46]

Next, understand what you know about your markets and clients. When the economic climate changes, what will be the impact on your primary clients' businesses? When a slowing economy changes your clients' business, there may be opportunity in assisting with downsizing or consolidations. Looking at current buying trends (e.g., projects, services, and fees) can help forecast new directions in client demand for your services.[47]

The Architecture of Value

An important metric to monitor is your hit rate (by sector or client type). What percentage of proposals written actually become new business, and how quickly? Equally important, but more subjective is your clients' satisfaction with your work. New business, or referrals, rarely comes from unhappy clients.

OPPORTUNITY KNOCKS (QUIETLY)

From this strategic analysis, you can start to determine the areas of best opportunity for your company. When these opportunities are in alignment with your firm's overall business approach, you can start to see what you should do differently. It can be as simple (or hard) as improving or increasing access to decision makers.

Often cited is the importance of developing new resources (both expertise and personnel). In the building industry, we often focus on professional networking with our peers, while our more successful competitors cultivate one-to-one personal relationships with the decision makers in our clients' markets.

How will you know when you are in a recession? If you wait for the government's latest prognostication, you will be late. Monitoring metrics that have an impact on your business and those of your clients is important. Are rents going up or down in your region? Are businesses failing (e.g., the dot-com collapse)? Is there investment capital readily available, or is there a reduction in venture spending?

An immediate indicator is a trend toward lower demand for your services. When there are fewer new proposals written or new project starts (month over month, quarter over quarter, year over year), or a decline in the scale, size, or duration of typical projects, it may be a sign of trouble ahead. The results of recessionary times are more competition, client downsizing, lower fees, liquidation of asset value, and industry-wide consolidation.

Economics

TAKING THE OFFENSIVE
The best offense is good defense. In recession proofing your company, the best strategy is to say no to work you know you should not do, and stay focused on core competencies. It is never too late to refocus energy on dormant clients (those you may take for granted).

Follow up on those less exciting, but usually profitable, stale leads that no one is tracking. Help clients create new assignments. Find ways to save them money, or to access money on their stalled projects. Looking at your clients' existing structure can often lead to recommendations for changes that may not have been evident to them.

Taking a more proactive approach through quality client relationships allows you to gain experience with a new project type (based on their satisfaction with your prior work). Similarly, using existing relationships to provide opportunities for a new or expanded geographic presence can help in uncertain times. In all cases, a consistent image and identity is important to developing, maintaining, and growing your market and establishing a sustained market position.

If your own recession analysis mandates a change in course, it may be time to hire new people with pre-existing business development networks in markets that can help grow your firm. More costly, but faster, would be to acquire a company with the skills or geographic presence you desire.

STRATEGIC RESPONSE
There are several main strategies to follow, whether in recessionary times or not. The first is to maintain a positive cash flow while achieving strategic goals. Look at trends regularly. Identify new and expanded services, but do not diversify unless necessary. Weed out bad clients, say no to bad deals, and avoid *ambulance chasing* that *mega-project* that has your sales staff drooling even though you do not have the resources or experience to do, nonetheless win, the work.

The Architecture of Value

Keep the clients you have by expanding services and helping them create new opportunities for you. Compete on value, not price, and learn to articulate *why*. It is important to be sensitive to pricing, but cheaper is not necessarily better. Make your services attractive and your projects profitable.

Becoming a connector with your network resources can help build alliances that will return the favor and include you in new project work as well. In an era of limited personnel, it is keenly important to retain key talent and hire strategically. A program that emphasizes the four "Rs" of human resource management (recruit, reward, retain, and retrain) should be a primary goal of your staffing efforts.

SURVIVING DURING A RECESSION is not much different from prospering during boom times. Look strategically at your business. Do not only focus on what you are doing now. Continue to market your services and monitor your clients' buying trends. Recessions do demand new services. Be creative. Follow the money. Most of importantly, be patient. Recessions do end and good times return on a regular, if not always predictable, cycle.

CHAPTER 20 | Identity

In an increasingly crowded marketplace, fools compete on price. Winners find a way to create lasting value in the client's mind.
Tom Peters

ONE MEASURE OF EXCELLENCE is the strength of your brand. With the trend toward alternative project procurement and delivery systems, the image of consultants in the minds of clients will undoubtedly change. Does your professional practice risk losing its identity, market share, or image, as clients expect project delivery from an integrated team, not an isolated firm?

While virtually every aspect of the new business climate is changing, and at an increasingly rapid rate, the answer is *"decidedly not!"* If your firm establishes its brand image within the marketplace, you will find your identity clearly realized and your business growing.

Excellence, like many *soft* assets of any business, is difficult to measure. It includes the knowledge base of your technical staff, the competitive spirit of your sales and marketing staff and, most importantly, the awareness and attitude of your clients to your services. A company's image and the resulting associations in the marketplace have a measurable impact on its ability to attract new clients.

The market's familiarity with a company's performance defines its brand equity. Used strategically, brand equity can be a prime source of competitive advantage and future earnings.

IDENTITY IS IMPORTANT
Develop a recognizable identity. A strong brand is not just graphical, but can be iconic. Your service quality defines your identity and results in your brand image. It should be consistent throughout your organization. Your marketing collateral materials only convey in words

The Architecture of Value

and pictures the quality and benefits your firm brings. The proof (and brand) is in the execution.

Your company name is important. This is simple, obvious, and often overlooked. Direct and easy to say, it should clearly define what you do. The finer you can define the service you provide, the easier it is for the client to understand how you can satisfy their needs.

Does a string of names of the firm's founders define your firm? Do they describe what you do? Develop a three to five word tag line for your business that helps the client remember you (and not your competition). A catch phrase may seem silly, but it is a proven element of contemporary brand development and can imprint your name in the client's memory.

I usually recommend avoiding acronyms. Alphabet soup does nothing to convey value. If based on the original founders' names, most people do not know what they stand for now, or stood for once. Companies like IBM and GE earned their acronym over time. You will, too, if your name conveys your value.

Be on the constant search for trends, prospects, and knowledge of who is competing in your market. Utilize local business associations, the chamber of commerce, and libraries. The Internet and its search engines offer the contemporary way to stay ahead of the curve.

Create a marketing plan that identifies your firm's vision and mission, sets realistic and achievable goals, outlines your objectives, and allows you to track your progress. Following and keeping the plan current is most effective. Knowing your marketplace and client expectations of perceived value is more important than knowing competitors' pricing strategies.

A current and comprehensive mailing list may be your most important weapon in the marketing arena. Frequent, direct (hardcopy or electronic) mailing campaigns and newsletters will keep you in front of

Identity

your targeted clients and prospects. Using first class postage allows returns and maintains the accuracy of the list. In addition, keep adding anyone you think should know about your work.

IMAGE IS EVERYTHING

The brand is the sum of all measurable and visceral characteristics—the idea, values, philosophy, features, and history that make it unique. The brand represents all internal and external assets—the people, name, iconography, literature, signs, and culture. It is anything and everything that influences how its target clients perceive the company.

According to marketing and positioning experts, brand image may be the best, single, marketable investment a company can make. Creating a positive brand image is a basic component of every business—the foundation for the future.

BUILDING THE BRAND

Companies like Coca-Cola (*The Real Thing*), Nike (*Just Do It*), and Apple (*Think Different*) each have a brand that is easy to remember. The brand identity generates positive associations. The goal of brand development is to make choosing to use your services easier. The brand represents the value and satisfaction your clients get working with you.

According to marketing and design consultant Stephen DuPuis, president of The DuPuis Group, "*The brand normally has to do two main jobs—first, to distinguish the company, and then, to differentiate the company from many similar ones in an appropriate, attractive, and legally protectable way.*" DuPuis also made clear the important difference between image and identity. He says, "*Image is the way a company is perceived by the public, and identity is how the company wants to be perceived. The brand is the intersection.*"

The Architecture of Value

The brand is more than a distinguishing logo associated with the firm's services. The brand reflects the quality of work associated with the firm's operations. If the brand is effective, it also differentiates those services from those of its competitors. A well-established brand identifies to the client the source of the service. It serves to ensure to both the client and service provider that competitors cannot provide services that seem to be identical.

Initially, brand equity builds by developing brand awareness. Through consistency of quality and service, this will form positive firm images in the minds of clients and ultimately yield high levels of brand loyalty. Brand equity in its simplest form is similar to what accountants call "goodwill." It is the inherent dollar value of the firm in the market, based on its history and success. By developing a strong and consistent image, established companies leverage their brand equity to give them measurable benefits.

MEASURING THE RESULTS

Establish and assess the value of your brand equity by reviewing three important, but subjective metrics.

- The **"price premium"** the name supports. Does the value of the service as perceived by the client enhance the service profitability?

- The **"impact"** the name has on client preferences. Does the name alone generate positive response?

- The **"replacement value"** of the brand. What is the cost, in time and money, of not using the brand?

These measures have a direct impact on criteria that are more tangible. Those include a company's stock market valuation (stock value less tangible assets) and the overall earning power of the brand. Brand

Identity

preference is the set of client beliefs that permits the brand to earn greater volume and margin than it could without the brand name.

KNOWING YOUR MARKET

Brand positioning relates to market segmentation. A good position is determined when you have divided the market into its particular segments and selected the target segments that best fit your services. Three issues determine brand position:

1. **What is your company's current position?**
   What does your market look like—what are the core competencies that define the dimensions in the market? What other firms are in that market and what distinguishes them? What are the unfulfilled segments or "holes" in the market? Which characteristics of your services are most important?

2. **What position do you want your firm to have?**
   It could be finding a client need not adequately met by the competition. Review your services' strengths that are unique and important. Determine the methods needed to correct weaknesses and thereby enhance your company's appeal. You may need to change your offerings to include different or additional services. By identifying market segments, you can focus on those that represent the best opportunities for your services.

3. **How do you create a new position?**
   The two basic ways to emphasize the company's differences are through targeted communications, and by creating memorable and meaningful ways that describe the firm's services. Marketing gurus Al Ries and Jack Trout point out, *"Positioning is not what you do with a product or service, positioning is what you do to the mind of the prospect."*[48]

The Architecture of Value

Brand positioning is an important strategy for differentiating your company's services. Positioning is the place that a company's services occupy in a particular market. A successful position has attributes that are both unique and important to consumers. Every company's services have a position.

Consumer perceptions, which may or may not reflect reality, define your position. Build your position by communicating a consistent message. Describe your services. Where do they fit into the market? A positioning statement tells someone, in one sentence, what business the company is in, what benefits it provides. Why it is better than the competition? Best, it causes them to say, *"Tell me more."* Imagine you are in an elevator and you have 30 seconds to answer the question, "What business are you in?" This is a good exercise to do with your staff. The variety of answers will surprise you.

THIS BRAND'S FOR YOU!

Brand development applies to any business, organization, or service. The techniques of branding provide a competitive advantage to the companies that use them. Conduct research with your clients and find the primary reasons that they buy your services rather than those of your competitors. Then use and repeat that message in every piece of collateral, press release, and in every interview. Every communication with your employees should reinforce your brand image.

THE MEANING AND VALUE of a brand resides within the mind of your clients. Without a unique brand, your company will not achieve its maximum revenue and profit potential. Moreover, in the world of professional services, your firm will have a harder time maintaining its position. To be effective, clients must see a reasonable link between their perception of your firm and the quality of your service. They must see the brand as the link between you and the excellence you deliver.

CHAPTER 21 | Referral

*There is no limit to what a man can do or where he can go,
if he does not mind who gets the credit.*
Robert Woodruff

THE RELATIVE EASE OF GETTING WORK is, more often than not, a direct function of excellence—the quality of service you provide your clients. It is always easiest to get new and additional services from existing clients than to sell new services in a new market to a new client. The key is quality client service.

In the view of many experts, your firm will have a culture based on quality only when your organization's basic beliefs and assumptions focus on the client, their needs, and desires. David Lindsey, AIA, Vice President for Nordstrom, one of the country's premier retailers, commented, *"The clients you want will pay a premium to receive extra value. This is the ultimate goal of client service quality."*

The easiest way to get new work is selling your existing services to your existing or past clients, or potential clients in the same market space. Providing *add-on* or expanded services to your existing clients is an excellent way to cement your long-term relationship, especially if you design those services in concert with the client's business needs. This is the very definition of *value-added*. Selling the same services to potential clients in the same market (i.e., that look like your existing client base) is somewhat harder, but not daunting.

Conversely, the hardest sale to close is *new* services to potential clients in a market you have not served before. In many ways, the esoteric nature of professional service can be a little like selling the ephemeral to strangers. In order for this difficult task to be successful, it takes patience, a commitment to educating the client, and a focus on service.

The Architecture of Value

LOOKING IN THE MIRROR

Admitting that your firm needs to improve its client service is often difficult. Few firms are willing to either admit or accept that, in their client's eyes, they need to improve. You might be surprised to find how often your services are *"over-promised and under-delivered."* In reality, you can improve your client service no matter how good you already are. Quality client service is a way of life.

Once you accept the need to improve, find out what your clients really feel. Do not assume you know. There are several ways to get this information. The simplest is to ask. You can also commission an independent client survey firm. Survey your clients and poll them for values that are important *to them*. Ask how your service compares to their expectations and to their experience with your competition.

Get input from both your best and most problematic clients, including potential clients. One of the key realities is that no two clients define quality the same way. More important is that they also define quality far differently from most professional service providers.

In the building industry, we pride ourselves on our ability to create innovative technical solutions. However, rarely do clients view technical quality as a quality service issue. Technical quality is a given—the cost of entry to your chosen profession. We all provide good technical service (well, most of us, anyway.). Therefore, if you think you can differentiate yourself on technical superiority, you are wrong.

DEFINING QUALITY

Developing a quality-focused practice requires an awareness of the following three observations:[49]

- Service quality is more difficult to evaluate than product quality.

Referral

- Clients do not evaluate service quality solely on the outcome of the service; they also consider the process of the service delivery.

- Clients define the only criteria that counts in evaluating service quality. Only clients judge quality; all other judgments are essentially irrelevant.

Looking outside the design and contracting industry for models is illuminating. The features of quality service that characterize successful businesses in other fields can be guidelines to improving your firm's delivery of service.

My observation is that clients care about service issues, listed in priority order:

- **Reliability:** Simply, this is doing what you say you will do. Perform as promised, dependably and accurately (not just with technical accuracy; this includes invoices, schedules, communications, etc.)

- **Responsiveness:** Willingness to help and providing prompt service

- **Assurance:** Creating a culture that focuses on your employee's knowledge, courtesy, and their ability to convey trust and confidence

- **Empathy:** Caring, personalized attention

- **Tangibles:** Expending the effort in the quality and appearance of your physical facilities, equipment, personnel, communication materials, and the deliverables that are the work product of your efforts

The Architecture of Value

Probably no single issue raises clients' ire more than poor communication. The simple act of promptly returning phone calls can build the client relationship. Conversely, failure to return calls weakens your credibility.

UPDATING PROCESSES

When you admit willingness to do something to improve your client service, you have assessed your client's perceptions, and your firm's leadership supports your mission, you will then need to evaluate all of the systems and procedures of your organization and begin to tailor your service goals and objectives.

Every practice is different—every service is unique. However, there are elements of awareness that they all share. The following steps can lead to implementation of quality client service as part of your firm's strategic plan:

- **Examine** your organization's mission as it relates to a client-service focus

- **Define** your vision of quality in your own terms, making it personal and motivational

- **Involve** everyone and every function in the firm in the process, from invoices to how you answer phone calls

- **Establish** a formal, active feedback process, talking to your clients about service issues throughout the project

- **Create** and emphasize training systems that focus on important non-technical skills like oral and written communications, active listening, interpersonal skills, and financial issues

- **Share** information with every member of your firm; the more awareness they have about client perception issues, the better they can respond

Referral

- **Eliminate** management or organizational objectives that conflict with improved service quality

Setting service quality goals requires three important steps. First, admit you have a problem or a need to improve your client's perceptions of your service. This admission must start at the top and be shared throughout the organization.

Quality is a cultural issue and takes time and effort by everyone to achieve. Second, define quality in the client's terms. Step outside your view of yourself. Seek truthful, objective feedback about what they value. Do not assume anything.

Finally, do something about it. Continually seek client input. Involve every process and person in your organization and share information freely. Focus on issues other than technical competence. Discard cultural notions that impair your ability to serve your clients.

DEVELOPING TRULY SATISFIED clients and a recurring list of referrals is a long-term commitment to excellence and a never-ending journey. You must accept on faith that the financial rewards will follow your improved quality client service. The results will be worth the effort.

The Architecture of Value

CHAPTER 22 | Network

People buy your music, not your words. Facts tell, but stories sell!
Brad Hager

WHAT IF YOU ADOPT A STYLE of marketing that would ensure a growing demand for your services. Would you also improve the professional skills and client-focus of all of your staff? Clients hire most firms because they serve an intrinsic business need. By building a network for your services, you can become *in demand* by potential new clients. They perceive your services as a need, and you do not have to sell.

Successful firms have networking programs that focus on leading edge services, while also placing a strong focus on training and development geared toward the core business opportunity associated with their business. Market expansion can come from either *warm market* relationships (i.e., the people you already know), but more likely is developed through *common market* connections (i.e., those potential clients who know your existing clients).

Similarly, they may know of you because they know your suppliers, sub-contractors, or affiliate businesses. Developing *hot market* relationships through client-to-client communication programs allows you to reach beyond your individual contacts.

You can build a culture based on a strong sense of community, enthusiastic recognition programs that celebrate both individual and group success, and a technology-enabled infrastructure. Almost any professional service can apply this new style of business development networking model.

VIRAL MARKETING

There is a lot of writing on the subject of viral marketing—the expansion of the awareness of a service through word-of-mouth or referral. The result of a viral effort is increased demand for your

The Architecture of Value

service. However, very few businesses are applying these concepts to their growth.

There are many analogies throughout history of how viral communication enabled growth, and how certain types of individuals (e.g., Gladwell's "Connectors," "Mavens," and "Salesmen") provide important linkages necessary to build market demand.[50] Identifying these key people is critical, but a regular discipline of relationship building is ultimately critical to success.

Author Seth Godin postulates that, counter to the conventional wisdom in marketing that attempts to control the dissemination of information in order to measure impact, the new business paradigm should focus on spreading information client to client rather than relying on only business-to-client dialogue.[51]

Contemporary network-oriented business developers use viral methods to great success by not only building client-to-client discourse, but by rewarding their client's loyalty and their referrals. They add a regular discipline of expansion of their message. They have as many people in the organization as possible present their service opportunity to three to five new *potential* clients each week.

They provide on-going, regular sales and marketing (and management and motivation) training for all of their associates in the firm. They leverage the power of positive affirmation. They expand their knowledge base through continual learning (e.g., subscribing to a business-oriented *book-of-the-month* program—and actually reading and applying the information learned).

Network

REAL-WORLD LESSONS
Four key elements to business success apply to any professional service firm:

- **Learn the business** – Ensure that everyone in your organization understands the fundamentals of your services, history, and vision. It is repeated often, but there is no substitute for having enthusiastic employees who are able to give a 30-second "elevator speech" that describes the value proposition of your firm—and are encouraged (and rewarded) for doing so wherever and whenever they can.

- **Do the business** – Make certain that everyone in your organization understands, and to the greatest extent possible, can articulate the roles and responsibilities of individual team members—whether principal, consultant, project manager, operations, or service staff. Cross training ensures that if there is an unexpected loss of individual talent there is the inherent ability to recover. This is especially true for "front-line" business development staff where relationships are important to success and loss of a rainmaker can lead to loss of future work.

- **Teach the business** – Build a learning organization that continually trains leadership development in the operational, financial, marketing, as well as technical aspects of the business. Some firms avoid this for fear of losing key employees, but successful organizations embrace building entrepreneurial spirit, knowing it will pay dividends more often than not.

- **Teach others to teach the business** – Create a mentoring environment that continually builds new teachers. This ensures that skilled employees understand more than just the technical fundamentals of their line role and train new employees. If business expansion includes starting new

The Architecture of Value

offices (or acquiring other businesses) to foster geographic or service growth, then existing staff will be better positioned to propagate your culture as you expand.

A NETWORK CULTURE

The most successful business people rely on a network of peers and associates and leverage that network to support and expand their companies. Consciously build a culture that trains, encourages, rewards, and celebrates each individual's abilities to build personal networks. That support of the business goals guarantees success.

Similarly, a culture that fosters both staff (all staff, not just marketing and business development) and client referrals through methods as simple as a "thank you" to more formal rewards (e.g., gift certificates, holiday gifts, time off, etc.) can generate new opportunities where none existed before. This has the added benefit of encouraging regular dialogue with past and current clients, keeping your firm *top of mind* for future work.

CONTAGIOUS ENTHUSIASM CHARACTERIZES most networking events (whether at your local Chamber of Commerce, Rotary Club, or industry trade association mixer). The process is by itself worth emulating. Building a *network* culture in your firm puts equal emphasis on individual efforts to expand their *net* in concert with the organization, as well as understanding the *work* of the business. Networking is a critical element for future success.

CHAPTER 23 | Impact

A leader is above all things an animator.
That is the essential condition of success.
Ferdinand Foch

TWO IMPORTANT ELEMENTS will help you develop business with your potential clients. The first is your proposal, and the second is your formal presentation. Each has special features that will help you differentiate yourself from your competitors.

Review the process and form you use to create proposals as you seek to improve profitability and earnings in your company. The quality of your proposals has an immediate impact on the closing rate of successful contracts.

THE WRITTEN WORD

Building industry pundit, Frank Stasiowski commented, *"The purpose of every proposal should be to get you the job, not just get you to the interview."*[52] Your proposed actions and capabilities should be at the forefront of the message. Every proposal should show the enthusiasm and energy that you put toward your projects. In most clients' eyes, that is more important than experience.

The best cover letter is concise, targeted, and client focused. The content should focus on the client's project, issues, needs, and hot buttons—and how you can uniquely address these. One thing to consider is whether you can address the client by their first name in the cover letter. Do you have that kind of relationship? Does your competition?

The first paragraph defines your approach to addressing the primary issue (who, what, when, where, or how) that will be critical to the project's successful completion, based on your market research. Avoid at all costs, *"We are pleased to submit..."* It is trite and adds nothing to

The Architecture of Value

indicate awareness of client issues. We are *all* pleased to submit. Hit them with something that will engage them in wanting to read more about how you can provide the solutions they need.

Words used in proposals should easily understood, sentences short and focused on clarity, and paragraphs limited to three sentences. Keep it simple; attack the challenge creatively. Include what you understand about their project.

The second paragraph describes, in no more than five bullet points, the how and why your approach to the project will be effective. Be sure that the points are relevant to their project and needs—do not recycle the same, tired "why hire us" bullets that could be found in any cover letter to any client for any project.

The final paragraph closes with any presumptions (start date, checklists, client input needed, etc.)—the tactical issues required starting the project. An assumptive tone (e.g., *"When the project begins, our first step is...,"*) says you are ready to start. Avoid "will" and "shall" and use language as if you are already on the project. Again, skip overused and insincere homilies (*"We look forward to working with you..."*).

Follow your signature with your contact information; make it easy for the client to get in touch with you. Your title should reflect your functional role on the project (i.e., project director, team leader, etc.), not your position in your company.

DEFINING THE APPROACH

Organize the content of the proposal in the same order as the client's RFP (request for proposal) or RFQ (request for qualifications). Number all pages. Use tabs and dividers to delineate major sections of the response. If the proposal is based from your contact with the client (i.e., self-generated), it should still follow a tabbed, section-based approach defining the major themes of your proposal. Typical sections include approach, scope, schedule, budget, team, and relevant experience. Use their words and their order *exactly* to look more responsive.

One way to differentiate your proposal from most others is to modify the traditional *executive summary* with a bulleted list (in the same order of the table of contents) that provides a simple summary of each major section and subsection. Simple factors like paper quality (24# minimum) and the contrast of color graphics (will they reproduce well on a B/W photocopy?) can have a subtle but significant impact on the reader. Study the graphic page layout. Does it provide large areas of white space—both for readability and for margin notes? Can you print double-sided to show your respect for the environment?

Is the font readable? It is easier to scan and retain sentences created in *serif* fonts like Times New Roman, Cambria, Palatino, Garamond, and Bookman. Font size should be large enough to be readable for eye at all ages. Make sure headers and footers are consistent and easily readable. Arial, Calibri, Century Gothic, Futura, or Helvetica are good choices for headers that stand out and help organize content.[††]

Testimonials (from happy clients) send a powerful message. Get them and use them (as large italic pull quotes including the reference's phone number) within the page design. Photographs allow readers to visualize your experience, proposed solutions, and approach. Make sure they are print quality (i.e., 300 dpi minimum) and consistent throughout the proposal.

Charts, graphs, and tables can summarize information at a glance and reinforce important points. Graphics also give the reader variety and breaks from solid pages of text. Reprints of published articles (focused on solutions similar to the client's) are also powerful third-party

---

[††] I designed this book using Century Gothic and Calibri for titles and call-outs, and Cambria for the text body.

The Architecture of Value

validations of your excellence. Include them as an appendix to your proposal or qualifications statement.

Your use of language has a significant impact on the reader's perception. Using words like "investment," "options," and "process" indicate value, choice, and thoughtful approach. They are much better than "cost," "alternates," or "scope." Your scope (*services* and *process*) should include a quantifiable checklist of deliverables. Tell them when and what input you need from them. Tell them what you will provide and how you communicate (e.g., email, voicemail, express mail, etc.). Explain what approvals you need at each major milestone to proceed.

Provide schedules, not just of time, but also of their investment over time. Show them in colored, bar-chart format the major milestones and tasks. Provide a cash-flow diagram showing everything they will spend over the time of the project (and beyond for service and maintenance).

WHO ARE YOU?

Resumes should be unique for each project. Include the individual's name, role, level of authority, and three projects describing their contribution to the project's success (in terms of the top issues relevant to the proposed project), with client references and phone numbers. Avoid all-encompassing paragraphs of years of experience, degrees, certifications, associations, etc. Summarize, if relevant, using bullets or a smaller font to the side or at the bottom of the resume. Be sure to notify anyone you use as a project or personal reference. Let them know what you want them to say, and request that if they get a call, they let you know.

When describing your firm's experience, be honest. Do not give the company credit for what your staff may have done before joining your firm. Do not claim credit for roles and responsibilities that were not really yours. After all, a simple question on these claims at the interview will sink the entire effort if you have over-reached. Do list and sort your experience in terms of the project's major issues (e.g., budget, schedule, function, process, services, delivery, etc.). Describe your capabilities as proven by experience.

GO FOR THE CLOSE
Several factors influence the buying decision a client. They are known as product, package, price, and place—the four "Ps" of marketing. The client sees the *product* (people, process, services) that you offer, the *package* (the image your proposal gives), and the *price* (their investment and the perceived payback). Equally important are the *place* your company has (versus your competition) in their mind. Adding a fifth "P," *promotion*—the influence of your marketing and communication efforts—can make the difference between you and your competitors.

Create a responsive, high-quality proposal that presents a unique (no filler) approach that addresses the specific issues important to the client. The increased revenue will recoup the effort many times over.

FACE TO FACE
If your proposal has the desired impact, a presentation will be the next step. For most professional service firms, this "short-list" process will allow you to present your credentials in formal settings—either on your own or as part of a team—to get the project. Understanding the issues of audience, team, content, visuals, and delivery can make a tremendous difference in your success rate. It can also help you communicate better with your clients.

KNOW YOUR AUDIENCE
People do not remember more than three to four main points. Keep your presentation tightly focused on the key issues. Your impression is made in the first 30 seconds—greet clients and audience at the door before you start, shake hands, and offer something (e.g., supporting handouts and leave-behinds).

The Architecture of Value

People hire (and work with) people they like. People tend to like those who are like them. Work on your attitude. People never read as carefully as you would like. Make sure you verbally emphasize the key points in your presentation (even if supported by visuals and bulletpoints). Similarly, people do not remember something they hear only once—or even twice. If it is important, say it *three* times—at different times during your presentation.

By the time you have been asked to speak, your expertise is a given—no need to be too nervous. More often, you offer a service that is so esoteric to the client that you will need to work hard just to simplify what you say about what you do.

KNOW YOUR TEAM

When you present as part of a group, several issues are important. First, choose team members early. This allows for strategy sessions on what topics will be covered, by whom they will be covered, and when during the presentation. This applies whether you are part of a panel on a common subject, or a member of a team representing your discipline.

Address the audience's important concerns. Cover the issues that are important to them. Respect protocol: if you are not the prime participant, do not interrupt. Let the team leader recognize you before you speak.

Limit the number of speakers in presentations. In some cases, team members may attend a presentation only to answer questions. Be sure your speaking team does not outnumber the audience. Rehearse, early and often, so that members of the team are comfortable with their part of the topic and place during the presentation. Make sure that your team members look at the person presenting. The client will be more likely to do the same.

Impact

CREATE THE CONTENT

Base your content on your goals—primary and secondary. Focus on your audience's needs and concerns. Make sure you define the "so what" for them in your presentation and answers. If your presentation is for a project, examine your strengths and weaknesses in relation to the competition. Articulate your point of view (based on your strengths and the client's needs).

Outline your presentation and check it for logical flow. Be sure you repeat your main points, providing variation on a theme. The standard approach is to tell them what you are going to tell them, tell them, and then tell them what you told them. A more effective approach is to tell them the *benefit* (what is in it for them), show them the *relevance* (why you are uniquely able to provide it), and provide them *proof* (where have you done this, or something similar, before).[53]

In addition, be sure to frame the presentation around the client, their project, and their needs. If it is not relevant to them, leave it out. Ask for action. Engage with the audience. Anticipate their questions. During your strategy sessions, brainstorm potential doubts and address those issues. Include the entire team, even those not attending the presentation.

PLAN THE VISUALS

Use no more than two visuals for every one minute of presentation time. Be sure they are relevant and appropriate for the audience and situation. Whether presentation boards, flip charts, computer graphics, video, or simple handouts, they should fit the size of room, size of group, and the image expected.

> **PERSPECTIVE**
> In the role of chief strategist for a technology integration company, I worked with the CEO to raise $20M in venture capital to fuel our growth—organically and through acquisition. That

The Architecture of Value

> process included many presentations to financial analysts and investment bankers. Because our work was somewhat esoteric, our presentation focused on the market opportunity and the growth characteristics of the overall industry sector. We reviewed our market share. We discussed why our services were increasing in demand. We demonstrated our differentiators.
>
> One of our advisors cautioned to tell our story in twenty slides or less. He commented, "Think like you are presenting to dogs. They are very smart dogs, but they are still dogs." Make sure what you say is clear, concise, and memorable.

Show only illustrations that help the client understand detail—not the overall complex issue. Emphasize a specific area of discussion with color or bold lines. Isolate and enlarge the details under discussion. Use your visuals to sketch your idea as you speak.

If you must use bullets, select three to five key words rather than full sentences. Limit each visual to no more than five lines. Visuals should support and enhance the message, so they must be readable: think about the audience and room size. They should not distract their attention from the speaker.

Better is to use metaphorical or illustrative images and a few words that speak to the core message. "Death by PowerPoint" has become so pervasive that many clients are specifying "no visuals" in their interview process. Avoid it by being creative, humorous, and inspiring. Keep them watching you, not the presentation. Include your company logo on first and last slides, but it is unnecessary on all images to reinforce your brand mark.

When you rehearse, use your visuals to get comfortable with them. Interact with them. Do not hide behind them. Worse, do not read them.

Impact

PRACTICE THE DELIVERY

Rehearse! Rehearse! Rehearse! Practice does make perfect. Plan several rehearsals and space them on the days before the presentation. Get coaching early in the process. Practice presentation timing between speakers as well as with transitions in content.

Consider involving others in your firm as "mock panels" to give feedback on the presentation and ask the team questions that the client is likely to ask. You can involve staff from all levels and departments as part of your learning culture.

> **PERSPECTIVE**
> In my experience as a Chief Marketing Officer, I tracked several hundred opportunities and projects. I found that when our teams met for an initial strategy session, established roles and the structure of the presentation, and the rehearsed, formally, at least three times, they were successful in winning the project more than 80 percent of the time. When they only rehearsed twice, the winning percentage dropped to 50 percent. When they opted to only rehearse once (or not at all), they only won 10 percent of the time. Practice makes perfect.

CONNECT WITH YOUR AUDIENCE

Get the audience involved. Talk with them beforehand; be in the room early. Ask them questions. They can be real or rhetorical. One option is to create your visuals as you speak. Flip charts and laminated site plans are great for this. Most important, be you.

Connect with your audience visually through:

- Eye contact
- Gestures
- Facial expressions
- Posture

The Architecture of Value

- **Movement**
- **Appropriate dress and appearance**

Pay attention to the vocal elements of delivery including your tone and the pitch of voice. Use variety. Watch out for non-words, jargon, acronyms, and technical terms only people in your business know. The audience will call you on it.

KNOW THE OUTCOME

When the presentation is over—debrief with your team and the client. It can be depressing to do something for which you have little potential success. At best, firms tend to have "hit rates" of 40 to 50 percent. More often, it's about 20 to 30 percent of projects awarded to total presentations made. Whether you win or lose, ask for feedback. It will give you ammunition for your next presentation.

Sometimes the client will award a project to a team even though your team submitted a great proposal and made an excellent presentation. Assuming you are targeting clients with long-term work potential, your positive impression will very likely help you. Look for an opportunity to reconnect soon after the presentation. Invest the time to continue to build a relationship. Learn what is next in their pipeline, and begin to position your firm to win. Your efforts will pay off.

THE POSSIBILITY OF WINNING a project with a client you have a relationship with is much higher than just relying on your proposal or presentation, notwithstanding the depth of your experience. Nonetheless, creating high-impact proposals and following good presentation rules are demonstrations of the excellence your firm can deliver for their project.

CHAPTER 24 | Technology

Information technology and business are inextricably interwoven.
Bill Gates

JAKOB NIELSEN, THE "GURU OF WEB PAGE USABILITY,"[54] predicts that client perception of *excellence* is the electronic interconnection between your business and your clients. Simply putting up a website brochure or offering e-mail connectivity is not enough.

Developing a long-term e-strategy will be a key element in any professional service practice. Clients expect access to greater amounts of information about your company and services, and faster response to their requirements for information and "bricks and mortar" solutions in a "clicks and mortar" virtual world.

In a reciprocal business environment, your company will need to gather and apply increasing amounts of data about your client's purchasing habits, as well as the client's short- and long-term strategies for growth.

We are in an era where the Internet's ubiquitous connectivity can help your businesses build stronger alliances between your clients, channel partners, vendors, and your staff. To manage the demand for immediacy, you will need a powerful and more interactive presence on the web. It should focus on your clients and their specific needs, and convey a strategic vision for e-based interaction that ignores the rules of the past.

PORTALS, HUBS, AND DESTINATIONS

It seems like only yesterday (in relative terms) that a simple website was all that was needed to describe your services, offer limited (please fill in our "guest book") interaction, to provide a connection between

The Architecture of Value

your business and a potential client. A retail site might include a modest transaction capability (i.e., a shopping cart).

Today, a third-generation site includes theme and metaphor that is creative and engaging. It has content that attracts new and existing clients, and has intelligence and customization. The site recognizes new visitors and offers unique information specific to their preferences.

Your web presence can be a portal, a hub, or a destination. Creating a "portal" was the buzz of the late '90s. A portal site's goal is to be the visitor's home page—the first site they see when logging on to the Internet. These sites provide guidance and navigation. Supported by advertising and some sales, they include content, search, services, personalization, as well as transactions. Sites like AOL, Yahoo! and MSN are classic portals.

Another site type is more akin to a "hub," (think axle, spokes, and wheel) providing content, information, and services through partnerships with other websites. Hubs are not as broad in focus as portals, nor do they aim to be a client's homepage. A hub has more sales and advertising information. Amazon is a good example of a hub site, aggregating information from many retailers and suppliers into one "store front." You may consider emulating similar business-to-business sites to aggregate your services with those of your consultants, contractors, and vendors.

A "destination" site provides a user with the ability to accomplish a specific task. Its content, information, and services focus on marketing information, sales, and client-specific transactions. In the building industry, *Globe Street* and McGraw-Hill's *Construction* websites are fine examples of destination sites. A corporate site could do well to provide this level and depth of pertinent information for a client seeking knowledge about the services of your company.

Technology

It is simply not enough to put up an informational brochure if you want clients to return to your site with any regularity. Content and relevance to the visitor's goals are the only assurance that they will continue to come to your site, will recommend your site to others, or will be able to find your site in the first place.

One crucial element for future success will be a website integrated with your transaction offering (a standard process and terms form), contract processing, and interconnected to your suppliers. Expert systems enable clients to make not only purchase decisions, but also have service-level interaction, providing *consultative* solutions based on user-defined needs and a common *rules* set that leads to a meaningful proposal and faster response. To stay ahead of your competition, think about developing "an app for that!"

SEEK AND YE SHALL FIND

With the deluge of new content and information available everyday on the web, it is a wonder that a potential client finds anything relevant that would land them at your site. Conversely, finding information on market trends, potential projects, and client-specific background takes an equal amount of (Sherlock) Holmesian persistence.

Most of you (and your potential clients) probably use one of the major search engines to find sites that contain the content you seek. The most popular tools for finding relevant information are the major search engines like Google, Yahoo!, and Microsoft's Bing. Getting to the "Top 10" on any search for you is critical.

As a result, search engine optimization has become an industry unto itself. If potential clients are going to find your business, you must promote your site to the major search engine. You should also imbed "meta" tags (key words) within your website. Think of these as the words most commonly used to search for your services.

The Architecture of Value

According to surveys at the website Search Engine Watch, more than anything else *links* to other sites on the site being visited are the major source of direction for potential clients reaching new destinations. This gives even more reason to have cooperative links with your vendors and supply-chain partners on your site (and theirs) so that your clients (and potential clients) will find and use your website as a useful tool.

E-COLLABORATION

There has been a marked increase in the use of alternative collaboration tools (e.g., videoconferencing and web-based conferencing). Many businesses have radically reduced travel by their staff, and work with their consultants and contractors using video and web-based technologies for project coordination.

Investing in videoconference equipment takes more than just purchasing hardware. To be effective, considerations of seating, lighting, and acoustics are critical. The concept of telepresence (pioneered by Cisco) takes traditional videoconferencing to a level of *"just like being there"* experience. Virtual meeting-space software providers also report major increases in the use of their web-based collaboration tools. Firms that embrace and apply this technology will have a big leg up (if it is marketed properly) on their competitors.

E-COMMERCE

An SMPS Foundation research study found that more than 70 percent of clients expect building industry firms to have client-accessible extranet and e-commerce (procurement/AR/AP) capabilities.[55] This is clearly the next wave of e-business in the service economy. Many clients already make connectivity the cost of entry for doing business with them (and the more robust the better). That is only going to increase as they build more tightly integrated enterprise knowledge processing systems for themselves.

Technology

As noted earlier, client relationship management and knowledge management systems are important to building effective, ongoing, high-value service relationships. It is also important to tie your marketing effort to the e-presence strategies of your firm. From promotion (on the web search engines) to constant and consistent content updates, to the form and format of true knowledge management, it is going to take a new breed of tech savvy marketer to keep your firm out in front.

E-EVERYTHING

Not as pervasive as in the retail sector, web-based transactions are having an impact on the building industry. No self-respecting consultant can avoid the need to participate without the risk of losing sales or appearing seriously out of date. At the end of the day, value-added services (like pre-design, feasibility, integration, service, and support) may prove to be more important than the price and convenience of any "Send-Me-a-Box (dot-com)" transaction-based web presence.

The successful company's e-commerce play will strengthen business-to-business relationships. They will develop affordable and accessible data, applications, warehousing, and information mining. Their clients will leverage one-to-one marketing's mass customization and build brand loyalty.

An evolving approach allows all participants in a truly shared value-chain to benefit from shared knowledge and the ability to predict demand and cost. Knowledge management tools provide integrated market research, targeted sales, and client service, combined with the order management, procurement, and financial systems. This process is likely to become the "killer-app" of the next decade.

The Architecture of Value

IP-EVERYTHING ELSE

The information technology industry is rapidly evolving the ability to utilize Internet Protocol (IP) addressing for device and system control in virtually every building and operations process. In the not too distant future, this will mean you will have the ability to control everything from building security, mechanical systems, lighting, elevators, etc., from your wireless-enabled cell phone. Similarly, overall network infrastructure is evolving to provide greater access to bandwidth and content with both wired and wireless nodes providing high-speed, high-resolution content.

Both clients and service providers benefit from computer networks that include the availability of many new and maturing technologies. The next generation Internet (aka, Internet2‡‡) will provide the ubiquitous bandwidth to allow us to develop new services that deliver higher value. Multimedia content is fast becoming an important component of client communication. The infrastructure needed to meet that expanding demand is quickly becoming available.

WHAT HAPPENS AFTER WHAT COMES NEXT?

Remember the words of Satchel Paige: *"Don't look back. Something might be gaining on you!"*§§ The only sure thing about predicting the future is remembering there is a future you do not see that could put you out of business.

---

‡‡ Internet2 is an advanced not-for-profit US networking consortium led by members from the research and education communities, industry, and government. In 2009, Internet2 member rolls included over 200 higher education institutions, over 40 members from industry, over 30 research and education network and connector organizations, and over 50 affiliate members.

§§ Leroy Robert "Satchel" Paige (July 7, 1906 – June 8, 1982) was an American baseball player whose pitching skills in the Negro leagues and in Major League Baseball made him a legend in his own lifetime, and equally known for his clever aphorisms.

Technology

Knowing what the future holds is not as important as knowing the future you want, and knowing that there are many influences on its outcome. In the words of James Collins and Jerry Porras, *"Building a visionary company is a design problem and great designers apply general principals, not mechanical lock-step dogma."*[56] Having vision is not the same as predicting the future. It is about having imagination, being true to your core values, and providing quality and value to your clients.

THE MORE THINGS CHANGE...

In 1995, I wrote a column for *Systems Contractor News*[57] magazine, where I reviewed of the use of on-line services as tools for business practice. Looking back, that perspective on the early applications of the Internet (e.g., e-mail, FTP, Usenet, etc.), the focus on proprietary bulletin board services, and the foundations of search systems (e.g., Archie, Gopher, etc.) seems quaintly antiquated.

Today "e-commerce" and "social media" are the watchwords for communication. "Sensors," "bots," and "expert" systems are the research tools of the future. In 2002, Jakob Nielsen suggested that soon you would have a range of new devices to interconnect your business with your clients, based on some implementation of wireless, high-bandwidth connection to the Internet that is always real-time and enables multimedia and other benefits. His prescient prediction predates the now ubiquitous smart phones. Moreover, Nielsen was making his predictions before Facebook was even an idea at Harvard.

THE SOCIAL NETWORK

Today, the number of popular social media networking services is growing rapidly, from Facebook to Twitter, Digg to Flickr, YouTube to Foursquare, Spoke to LinkedIn—and on and on and on. You can barely turn on your computer without finding some new place to share information, post your profile, and interact with friends and colleagues. The trend is too big to ignore, and certainly too big to stop. Social media

The Architecture of Value

presents both an opportunity for client connection and an ever-increasing challenge to manage in the workplace.

In 2011, the statistics for Facebook alone are mind numbing. The number of Facebook users, at 600+ million, would rank third in population in the world (of 221 countries) and ahead of the United States in fourth place. Users spend more than eight billion minutes and post more than 45 million status updates on Facebook daily. More than ten million users "like" a new page each day.

Clearly, social networking sites are part of the culture and growing. However, many users are unaware of the risks of divulging personal information or have limited understanding of the potential threats. Businesses should take technological safeguards, educate users, and establish policies for access and use of social networking services. Today, about 50 percent of businesses use firewall software to block access to Facebook and MySpace.

SOCIAL MEDIA PITFALLS

The top reasons for restricting access to employees' ability to "surf" to any location on the Web include:

- Virus and spyware prevention
- Employee productivity drain
- Bandwidth concerns
- Liability concerns
- Employee downloading

Industry analysts acknowledge that the greatest threats to business from social media access are:

- Digital dossier aggregation
- Secondary data collection

Technology

- Face recognition
- Content-Based Image Retrieval (CBIR)
- Linking from image metadata
- Difficulty of complete account deletion
- Spam

Other key risk issues that should be considered are cross-site scripting (worms, viruses); phishing (the criminally-fraudulent process of attempting to acquire sensitive information such as usernames, passwords, and credit card details by masquerading as a trustworthy entity in an electronic communication); network hacking and infiltration; ID theft; stalking; and bullying. Other potential social media pitfalls include lack of productivity, negative publicity, discrimination, harassment, defamation, and loss of proprietary information.[58]

SOCIAL MEDIA BENEFITS

Despite the risks, there are many benefits to giving employees access to and encouraging use of social networking services:

- Instant contact with others
- Great information source/resource
- General awareness/enhanced branding
- Relevancy ("everyone is doing it")
- Effective employee recruitment

Further, using blogs, tweets and tweet chats, Facebook business or fan pages, LinkedIn business group pages, etc., provides yet more venues to promote the excellence of your practice. Social media is another tool for employee recruitment and shows great promise for communicating value to your client base.

The Architecture of Value

DEVELOPING A POLICY

At a minimum, a well-defined social networking policy should include:

- "Scope of Regulation" (e.g., during work hours, if at all)
- Disclaimers and warnings
- Use of company logo and other brand-related information

The policy should disclose the employer's right to monitor activity while at work. Tie the policy to other policies like harassment and confidentiality.[59]

In addition, the policy should restrict publication of negative, confidential, or proprietary material and outline the consequences. Further, the policy should define the employee's appropriate scope of use for computers (e.g., is personal use permitted?) for email, web surfing, and social media posting.

It also should address issues of discrimination, posting references or comments about the company, unauthorized access to restricted sites, and violation of privacy or free speech rights. A good policy will also reference existing email policies and the use of smart phones and PDAs as alternatives to the employees' workplace computer, and extend to both business and personal blogs.[60]

Having a policy for use of social networking within the business environment is a challenge every business needs to face. Many are embracing social networking by creating business pages on Facebook and LinkedIn to promote their company to potential clients and encouraging employees to use the site to celebrate successes and promote the business to potential new staff. Social media's advantage is creating an ever-increasing network. This has too many upsides for business growth to ignore. Address the downsides with a thoughtful policy, open dialogue, and employee education.

Technology

THE GROWING IMPORTANCE OF UNIFIED COMMUNICATION, regardless of media, will be based on mobility, allowing new services to be accessed anywhere at any time—what you want, when you want it, and how you want it. Your network of social media connections will further your ability to reach a larger audience. Moreover, the same will hold true for your clients. Investing in and developing *excellence* in all aspects of e-service is critical to the development of the enduring practice.

The Architecture of Value

CHAPTER 25 | Results

*However beautiful the strategy,
you should occasionally look at the results.*
Winston Churchill

IS YOUR MARKETING PROGRAM DELIVERING VALUE? Do you ever feel like you are wasting money? Unfortunately, most professional service firms do not track return on their promotional efforts. The good news is that there are simple steps you can take to ensure that your investment in marketing is paying off.

There is confusion about what encompasses "marketing." For purposes of this discussion, marketing is different from sales. It includes all the tools used to communicate information about your firm to existing and potential clients. Marketing includes research, planning, public and media relations, and information management. Your sales or business development personnel deliver that message, but the marketing department develops the strategies and message and organizes, plans, and evaluates the effectiveness of the communication.

EFFECTIVE METHODS
There are many methods used to market professional services. Some of the most popular include:

- Advertisements
- Awards programs
- Brochures and proposals
- Direct mail
- Email
- Professional directories
- Sponsorships

The Architecture of Value

- **Websites**

However, an SMPS Foundation research survey of consultants showed that *the most effective methods* included:

- **Educational Seminars**
- **Community Involvement**
- **One-on-One Meetings**

This highlights the importance of direct communication with clients and prospective clients. While marketing materials can help in building brand recognition, position, and perceived value, you still need face-to-face contact to build relationships.

Most firms do not produce client-centric materials. Search your own brochures, qualifications packages, or proposals for the terms *"I," "we," and "our."* Effective communication focuses on the benefits to *"you," "your,"* and *"their."* The client will always be more receptive to how you can solve their problem, and more so, how you have solved similar problems in the past.

It is important to provide both clarity and excitement in your communication. Enthusiasm is a great tool to excite the client about working with you. Defining what is unique and different about your firm, your services, and your people is equally important. Most firms share common history (*"We've been in business for 'X' years."*), experience (*"We've completed 'X' projects."*), and tools (*"We have state-of-the-art 'X' systems."*), so look for something new to say that sets you apart. What can the client get from you that they can get nowhere else?

Keep your message simple (short words, short sentences, short paragraphs, and great pictures). Keep it concise. Think: *"You have 15 seconds to tell your story. Go!."* Think bumper stickers. Make it relevant (timely and honest). Know your market (and the client's hot issues).

Results

SURVEY SAYS?

Client surveys can be an effective tool in measuring the subjective side of marketing ROI. It is never too early to start asking questions and tabulating data. Develop a systematic approach to query the client at various stages (both pre-sale and post-sale, during the project, and even post-project completion). Use that information strategically to improve your message. Learn to ask. Learn to listen. Learn to act on the information they give you.

Client feedback will consistently differentiate between the poor (*"I won't work with them again."*), the best (*"They are a great firm to work with."*), and the truly superior organization (*"I love working with them."*). Lost in the middle (*"They're OK."*) is everyone else.

Rank you firm using the following subjective metrics and set up a plan to move up the list.

- **Superior**
  - Never fails to meet strategic service requirements
  - Understands client's business objectives and expectations and consistently exceeds them
  - Raises client expectations by delivering additional, innovative, value-added services

- **Best of Class**
  - Never fails to meet service requirements
  - Understands project-specific expectations and exceeds them
  - Sometimes delivers additional, value-added services

- **Just Another Face in the Crowd**
  - Meets service expectations
  - Meets service requirements
  - Never surprises client with new services

- **To Be Avoided**
  - Inconsistent in service delivery
  - Fails to meet service requirements

The Architecture of Value

- Responds poorly to service failures
- Delivers unpleasant surprises

Congratulations to those who think they are already "superior," but make sure you have the strategies in place to stay there.

OTHER MARKETS

Surveys of non-building industry service firms show that most (more than 50 percent) have some method for measuring marketing ROI. However, most building-related organizations (more than 75 percent) do not. Measuring ROI on marketing is a multi-dimensional process.

Developing a marketing ROI system requires you to:

- **Know what you want to measure.** Agree on simple metrics at first; expand as you build the process.

- **Know how you are going to measure.** Set up systems to record, tabulate, and sort the required information.

- **Create a plan and follow through.** Communicate and train all of your staff on the importance of participating in the project and communicate on-going results.

- **Measure against expectations.** Check at regular intervals against assumptions, look for anomalies, and adjust the process.

- **Formalize the process.** Make it a regular part of your business plan.

Building a database of relevant marketing history should include:

- **Leads:** sources of referrals, direct sales, direct marketing, indirect marketing, PR, etc.

- **Expenses:** all related direct and indirect costs associated with marketing and project development

- **Revenues:** resulting revenues from all services

Results

- **Opportunities:** preliminary project-specific interest in your services

THE BENEFITS TO YOU

By formalizing and making routine the process of measuring, you can quickly build a database of experience. This storehouse of both objective and subjective (anecdotal) information helps you map, track, and direct the evolution of the client relationships you are trying to build. Look for trends upward or downward.

Use a 12-month trailing average to give a "barometric" view of long-term trends to check the temperature of the market and your performance. Measured data should include month-over-month, quarter-over-quarter, and year-over-year comparisons of averages for:

- **Number** of proposals written
- **Dollar value** of proposals written
- **Client sector** (e.g., business, education, or government; the segment you use will depend on your business type and focus) **economic industry indexes**
- **Number** of interviews
- **Number** of wins (i.e., hit ratio) as a ratio of proposals written *and* interviews
- **Cost** per proposal (overhead and expense)
- **Incremental expense** and return on investment (ROI)

IT DOES NOT count if you do not count it. The only way to justify new or continued marketing expenses is to develop an accurate and relevant measure of ROI. You may be surprised at the results, but the benefits to your organization will be focus on client service and satisfaction. In the end, that is all that matters.

The Architecture of Value

PART III | Grow Your Practice: *Deliver* Experience

Happiness is not something you experience.
It is something you remember.
Oscar Levant

EXPERIENCE COMES FROM THE "RIGHT PRACTICE" of your practice—providing work that people love to do, and as a result, work that your clients love to experience. Positive experience brings clients back for more service, but negative experience sends them running to someone else. The elements of experience in a professional service practice include all those *day-to-day* aspects of delivering on the promise of the elements of expertise (design) and excellence (market). They are often some of the most mundane, but always some of the most important aspects to building an enduring practice.

As the professional service industry evolves, you will need to recognize that, in the words of author Jim Gilmore, *"Experiences are as distinct from services, as services are from goods and products."*[61] The elements of experience define the cultural and operational aspects of the business. The consequences define your future.

CULTURE
Creating a service firm that both values and enables its people is one of the cornerstones of long-term success. Recognize the benefits of mentoring and training. Provide an interesting and *fun* environment in which to work. This goes a long way to foster loyalty. Employees, who with grace and gratitude recognize that these benefits are not an entitlement, but an advantage, are more likely to mature into the leaders of tomorrow.

The Architecture of Value

INTEGRITY
Mutual respect, efficient operations, and cost-effective results characterize long-term relationships. Satisfied clients will shop anywhere. Loyal clients will recommend you to others and will rarely switch. The easiest way to get loyalty is to give it. Act as if you are part of their company and culture; think as if you were on their staff.

Ultimately, you can overcome the focus on individual importance and selective, self-serving, and myopic views. Understand that constructive collaboration and a team-based approach to project implementation will be of greater benefit and experience to all involved.

MANAGEMENT
Projects define the experience between your practice and your clients. Project management is the key to planning and executing the vision of the design. Empowered project managers present a responsible approach that meets the needs of each client and delivers a positive experience. Well-managed projects are the foundation of profitable professional practice.

TEAMWORK
Collaboration between service provider and client is a key to building long-term, enduring relationships. Working in the client's best interests requires a keen understanding of the economic, business, and organizational trends in their industry. Becoming expert in their business translates into a positive experience for both parties; you improve your ability to offer services to a larger market and they, in turn, receive the highest quality service.

OPPORTUNITY
Healthy, long-term contracts and recurring revenue streams are the Holy Grail for all professional services. Building client relationships around the elements of contractual strength is one of the keys to

delivering a positive experience. Recognition that you are in business to succeed (not just survive), and that profitability is not an oxymoron for your service firm, is an important step to building an enduring practice.

AGREEMENT
Developing healthy contracts that are mutually agreeable and beneficial requires the acceptance of your staff—particularly your project managers—that your position is not in conflict with the client's self-interest. Follow common sense rules during the life of a project, communicate change, and recognize that there are always two (or more) viewpoints. This is a skill, once mastered, that helps generate a positive experience for all.

NEGOTIATION
Change happens. Anticipate this potential. Maintaining contractual standards is important to the experience of the project. Understanding the process of negotiation—when to stand firm and when to bend—is one of the important steps in building a professional practice.

DIALOGUE
Meetings are a necessity. They can also be a waste of time. A well-planned and properly executed meeting leads to improved dialogue and communication. Understanding their benefits and knowing how to best organize, manage, and contribute is one of the key elements of the project experience.

COMMUNICATION
Perception is often reality. The responsibility for communicating options, opportunities, and dangers falls squarely on the shoulders of the service provider. Enabling a positive experience through proactive communication can help build a strong relationship that leads to ongoing work.

The Architecture of Value

CHALLENGE
Every project begins with a vision. Clients and consultants presume the work be provided on time and on budget. Ideally, it will exceed expectations for quality. Unfortunately, not everything goes as planned. Failure to fully communicate, outside influences, or unintended consequences of other actions can all have an impact on the success of a venture. A consultant who approaches these inevitable challenges, develops solutions, and communicates the process openly always creates better outcomes.

EVOLUTION
The evolution of a professional service practice necessitates responding to new and changing building industry dynamics. Applying your expertise to new service delivery methods requires an open mind and willingness to collaborate with not only your peers and clients, but sometimes, with your competitors.

DELIVERING A POSITIVE AND MEMORABLE EXPERIENCE is probably the most difficult theme to master. It requires the most attention and garners the fewest accolades. Building an experience-focused firm comes from the design and marketing efforts, and represents the best of your expertise and excellence. *Experience* is the all-important last leg of the proverbial *three-legged stool* on which your future ability to grow rests. Focus on the following elements of *experience* will help you reach your goal.

CHAPTER 26 | Culture

Changing the culture means changing the habits in your organization...
Peg Neuhauser

THE SINGLE BIGGEST CHALLENGE in a professional service practice today is finding, developing, and keeping good employees. Every business manager's goal is to build a workplace that provides staff with great projects, clear processes and expectations, and opportunities for professional growth and learning. The result is increasing profitability (providing value to your shareholders and stakeholders) and, if all goes well, having *fun*. A positive culture delivers a positive experience to your clients.

Projects include principals, business developers, marketers, designers, project engineers, project managers, programmers, specialists, technicians, operations, and client service staffers. We all want to work on great projects, excel at our craft, and know what is expected. We all want to create satisfied clients (internally and externally), continue to learn more and earn more (paid for our value) and, if all is going well, have *fun*.

The more pragmatic reality is that you often have more mediocre-to-good projects than you can possibly handle. You are under-staffed, making the process of completing that work a challenge for the too few available to do the work. You have little or no time for real training, let alone developing new skills and responsibilities.

There is an increasing demand from clients for faster delivery of increasingly complex projects. They expect a high level of service causing almost immediate conflicts. Their expectations result in more time spent to get to the satisfaction level they require. To reach effective completion, you spend more time. As a result, you

The Architecture of Value

compromise profitability in favor of closure. You have less money to use for growth, rewards, or sharing. Are we having *fun* yet?

Statistics show that professional service firms will find fewer and fewer graduates entering the industry. With a plethora (or lack) of work and a shortfall in staff, employers use any effort to seduce new staff from competitors. With high demand, good employees are looking twice at any opportunity to move, and, unfortunately, on average they are taking it. You face a choice between "company man (or woman)" or what *Fast Company* refers to as a "Free Agent Nation."[62] Which path leads to building the successful workplace of the future?

A MESSAGE TO MANAGEMENT

Rosabeth Moss Kanter, professor at the Harvard Business School, commented, *"You can't buy loyalty with just a paycheck. Building long-term commitment depends on four things: The nature of the work, the opportunity to grow, the chance to speak up and be listened to, and the feeling of making a difference."*[63]

Building a sustained, competitive advantage takes more than just focus on profit and loss. It takes an unwavering focus on people. Kanter noted that companies like Cisco Systems and Southwest Airlines have built organizations that are models for both corporate growth and employee-focus. Management needs to demonstrate—everyday—a commitment to personal development (training, continuing education, certification), and recognition that lifestyles require flexibility (single parenthood, relaxation, and recreation).

Client-customized projects have logistics challenges light-years beyond the '40s and '50s era assembly-line factory. Baseline business requirements of excellence in cash management, documenting processes, and measuring and reporting results are the minimum cost of entry. Leadership, team building, celebrating, and rewarding (staff and clients) are the requirements to create a profitable future.

Culture

Kanter went on to say, *"Members of the new generation in the work force don't want to be subordinates; they want to control their own fate. They want to do meaningful work that has redeeming social value without sacrificing the chance to get a life. Give them that and they'll give you loyalty in return."*[64]

A MESSAGE TO EMPLOYEES

Tom Peters voiced a slightly different perspective: *"I want my company to be so attractive, so laden with talent, so energetic it makes your head swim. I want to give you an exciting work environment, peerless teammates, and a string of challenging projects with top clients you could not match anywhere else. In turn, I demand that you give your all to these hot projects. Moreover, I demand that you be loyal—to your teammates, to the client, to yourself. You must perform and grow as you've never performed or grown before."*[65]

I think this is an important point. You work every day in teams on projects. It is the nature of the professional service business model. Those teams include management, marketing, design, engineering, operations, and other service "players." There are superstars, journeymen, and rookies in each part of the team. Nevertheless, the *team* completes the project. The *team* satisfies the client.

Effective leaders look first to building, supporting, and strengthening the organization that supports the team—at the expense of their personal gain or notoriety. Real leaders—those who will build the companies of the future—strive to create Peters' "WOW" workplace where these great projects are the everyday reality.

Those people who jump from job to job just for the bump in the paycheck (or the next signing bonus) will not grow personally or professionally. At some point (usually sooner than they think), they will become valueless to the team that needs proven partners, not just players in a shell game.

The Architecture of Value

Peters qualified his view, saying, *"I also demand that you not be 'loyal' to me or my company. I do not want you to stick around out of misguided allegiance. If I can provide you with exciting new challenges, and if you respond accordingly, well then I hope you and I do indeed grow old together—one project at a time."*[66] Moreover, I add: one *team* at a time.

BUILDING VALUE

In this age of new practice models and innovative startups, it is hard to imagine a future for business that is not exciting and ripe with the challenge and opportunity you desire. However, there can be no future unless company leadership recognizes and supports the value of the individual, and that the individual recognizes that they have a personal and professional obligation to help develop the company that they want to work in.

LASTING PROFITABILITY is the result of good work. Individuals who focus on *get rich quick* will not be the leaders of the successful companies of the future. Companies that do not construct pathways for ongoing personal and professional development into the manifestation of their business paradigm will not be able to hire or retain good employees. Those who work to build their organizations and those who celebrate those contributions will be laughing all the way to the bank.

CHAPTER 27 | Integrity

Integrity without knowledge is weak and useless, and knowledge without integrity is dangerous and dreadful.
Samuel Johnson

ON MORE THAN ONE OCCASION, I witnessed a classic project dilemma. In the quest for the ultimate experience, someone conceded to the client's desire for a *"state-of-the-future design."*

Unfortunately, that goal of providing (and the ability to achieve it) an advanced level of functionality was not readily available. Then the consultant faces a challenge. Does the designer travel the safer path and provide a conventional solution? That approach may meet current needs with proven materials and tools, but does not achieve the client's vision for the project.

Whether integrator or consultant, this challenge is at the core of your capacity to advance the science of professional service. The right answer presumes a level of integrity that would have the practitioner offer the client an open and honest assessment of both the risks and rewards that such options offer. This also presumes your firm can document project concepts in functional, executable specifications that allow for accurate cost analysis and the ability for the integrator to execute your design.

THE SEDUCTION OF THE UNKNOWN

On one hand, the seduction of utilizing untried (and even unavailable) systems or components is great. It provides a chance to push the envelope and test new concepts. If it works, you may gain a level of professional credibility and praise for trying and realizing a new idea. When creativity meets willingness to risk, the opportunities for innovation are unlimited.

The Architecture of Value

Even with existing processes, there are others in the project loop that will have an impact on the results. These outside influences can be either an aid or hindrance. It is important to remember that you do not work in a vacuum.

AN ACT OF CONVENIENCE

Unfortunately, we seem to live in a time when, for either profit or pride, there is a too often an easy acceptance of what might be called *situational ethics*. This is simply a convenient adjustment of one's view or actions at a given time to serve personal goals—more often than not, at the expense of others. This leads to promises for solutions that are at best misleading. They presuppose that someone else will figure out a methodology to build the notional concept.

When you cannot build it, where does the fault lie? The practitioner of situational ethics will always insist that it is someone else's problem. Whether it is a client that did not understand, another consultant who did not listen, someone else who thought they could do it better, or an integrator who could not figure out how to make it work, the responsibility is never theirs.

RESOURCES FOR INPUT

A group of inter-related decision-makers in areas of organizational vision, project implementation, and end-user applications represent the client. Consultants of all disciplines interpret their needs. Integrators and contractors implement the design. The integrators rely on manufacturers and suppliers to deliver components. This synergy is the means by which you meet the client's *functional* and performance requirements, and project goals for budget and delivery.

When integrity of purpose is missing and ethics are compromised anywhere in this process, the results are more than likely to cause dispute. The magnitude can range from minimal to catastrophic. Ego

Integrity

and self-indulgence cause more damage to all industries than we care to admit.

AGAIN AND AGAIN

Do not add unnecessary components while representing that this approach improves the client's environment (your penultimate goal). Such designs are ill conceived, whether for simple greed, or perhaps worse, the mistaken belief that *"more is better."* Adding redundant complexity more often than not does the entire project great disservice.

Nicholas Negroponte insightfully notes, *"Redundancy is generally considered a bad symptom, implying needless verbosity or careless repetition."*[67] More often than not, failure to recognize that less is often more results in clients with a view that certain potentially useful solutions are unreliable, expensive, or un-workable.

A HIGHER STANDARD

Fortunately, most of the professionals recognize and support that we need to raise the bar for the delivery of the service. We must insist that those in professional service developing new solutions and applications create systems that actually meet the client's need, not just the consultant's vision.

Hold manufacturers to task for marketing promises that claim to solve problems they do not quite answer. Integrators need courage to challenge flawed design specifications. A client informed and satisfied with a successful project is worth much more than just the chance to bid on future projects. Without that level of integrity, disputes and adversarial attitudes arise and cloud the working relationships for all involved in the project.

Many industries have begun to address these issues through learning requirements that may mitigate some of the problems. Mandatory continuing education and solution-specific certification programs are

The Architecture of Value

an excellent start. The professional service community's support for these initiatives is critical.

TO COMPETE IN THE GLOBAL MARKETPLACE, you must be able to demonstrate advanced technical skills, excellent communication abilities, and multi-disciplinary harmony. The professional service industry represents a major percentage of the U.S. Gross Domestic Product and an equally large portion of the global economy. We are all significant players in the next age of business practice. The ability for professional services to evolve to a higher level is dependent on your willingness to focus on integrity and ethics.

CHAPTER 28 | Management

The definition of management is getting work done through people, but real management is developing people through work.
Agha Hasan Abedi

PROJECT MANAGEMENT IS IMPORTANT to effective organization, staff and resource allocation, progress, and cost control. Both consultants and contractors undertake dozens of projects for their clients annually and each has project management needs and definitions that can vary considerably from office to office.

Project management systems create a structure. They help make sense of potential chaos and communicate status and headway to both the client and firm management. A correctly managed project is continually *"choosing to do the right job before doing the job right."*

There are numerous systems available as resources to help guide project management within your firm. However, understanding some basic precepts is important to assist those project consultants who perform the project management function. Most companies do not employ professionally trained project management specialists.

It is important to know the difference between project cost control and project management. Project cost control is only one part of a company's overall project management process. Financial-accounting system job costing is a historical report of *yesterday's* performance. Project management functions are determining the affect on the future of today's decisions and planning tomorrow's performance. *"You can't see the future through the rear view mirror."*[68] The closer to real-time the information you review, the better you are able to take immediate corrective action.

The Architecture of Value

Managing a project involves the critical planning and monitoring of time for all personnel. To hold a project manager responsible for project results, give them the responsibility and authority to control resources. In addition, a project manager should have a keen sense for the schedule and logistic needs, tempered with a sense of urgency.

Many technical people lack the business skills necessary to manage complex efforts to complete them on time, and at or below budget. Select a project manager who has an appropriate personality and affinity with the client and their staff.

EMPOWERING THE MANAGER

It is critical to provide full authority to the project manager to control and manage the project. Include project managers at the proposal, negotiating, and planning, as well as the implementation stages. Do not negotiate any fee without finishing the project budget.

The project manager should carefully review the proposed project contract. Make sure there is a clear statement of the scope of work, project schedule and budget, operational procedures, provision for changes and extras, reimbursables, and form(s) of payment.

If it is not a standard contract for your office, make up a checklist for use in analyzing the new terms. To inform the team of key schedule and task elements of a new project, write up and document each salient major project event in clear concise language.

Regular reporting systems are very important. If a project continues to slip in both time and budget until the phase is well toward completion, you may have to throw people and money at the job to undo the delays and work your way out of the accumulated problem.

Review the project's progress frequently. Use computer-based scheduling tools to provide timely and accurate results. Monthly reports on small- to medium-sized projects are inadequate. You can get

Management

into too much trouble in 30 days (plus the internal paper turn-around time). Weekly or bi-weekly information is better.

Do not overload your project managers. Know the proper balance for your discipline, types of projects, and experience. Base your decisions on a combination of project dollar value, number of managed personnel, and years of experience.

Your firm should have a project manager's manual. Many firms say that the process of writing it was as important as the final document. Do not use an outside consultant. Give the job to the best project manager in the firm and give him or her maximum support. Set up a schedule and stick to it. Otherwise, momentum and interest will wane. As a result, they will never finish the manual.

Much of a project manager's work is communicating with other people about the project. The project manager should employ effective people management techniques. Emphasis should be on communication between and among all project staff. Hold regular project meetings to ensure this.

Delegate decision making to administrative support staff to reduce interruptions—let your primary support person know your to-do list so they can help—make sure they know your functions, responsibilities, and activities, both inside and outside your company.

The "excess perfection syndrome" is a significant contributor to project delay and overrun costs. For example, this might be an unnecessary effort to improve a report, analysis, specification, etc., by spending 10 to 15 percent more time to achieve only a 3 to 4 percent improvement. Know when to blow the whistle on over-designed tasks.

The Architecture of Value

WHEN PROBLEMS ARISE
What do you do for projects behind schedule? While these suggestions may not work on every job, they have proven themselves over time:

- **Check the project contract.** Ensure you are only delivering required tasks, on the original schedule, and within the agreed upon budget. Review each of these three areas to discover additional services.

- **Work overtime.** Complete the assignment and move staff back to profitable work as quickly as possible.

- **Change staff work assignments.** Put more experienced or efficient personnel in charge of completing the work. Bring the firm's principals on the job. Roll up your sleeves and get back in the trenches bringing experience (and mentoring) to overtaxed staff.

- **Bring in temporary staff.** Outsource to complete the project quickly.

- **Reorganize and simplify the work.** Ensure that you are not over-delivering beyond the detail needed to convey design intent and integration requirements.

- **Think about what the client can do to expedite the job.** Do not work in a vacuum. Make the client aware of the issues and collaborate in developing a mutually satisfactory solution.

After every major project is completed, have a team debriefing to discuss "lessons learned" from the experience. Include the client and representatives from all other team members.

- **Was the project profitable?** If not, why not? If so, could you have made more?

- **How did the team work as a team?** Could you improve communication?

Management

- **Evaluate the client.** Would you want to work for them again? What do you need to do to get more work from them?
- **Review how you handled your resources** (people, time, and money) **on the job.** Did you do a good job? Did you over-use the resources?

Project success is the result of successful technical and project management personnel. Because no project starts with a perfect schedule or resources (and real-world events would mess them up even if they did), a focus on project management skills is critically important to project profitability.

EFFECTIVE PROJECT MANAGERS use early planning, consistent monitoring, and communication to succeed. Because of this, their contribution to a project is as important as the technical design. That contribution is the heart of the experience that will determine if the client is satisfied, happy, and loyal.

The Architecture of Value

CHAPTER 29 | Teamwork

If an opportunity doesn't knock, build a door.
Anonymous

ONE OF THE TOUGHEST CHALLENGES in a slowing economy is to convince clients to start a project. Plans for new projects or changes and updates to existing systems are often the first put on hold or cancelled when the client's own market starts to contract.

What can you do to stimulate your market, clients, and clients to get them to continue to see the value of your services, resulting in new and continued business growth? For firms to succeed in the *new normal* economy, you must move away from traditional one-off, transactional thinking toward a more collaborative approach.

Critical to the long-term growth of a consultancy is the ability to deliver services to existing clients that result in recurring revenue. One way is to convince them that increased productivity comes from the results of your efforts. That is the message most of the proactive firms practice and present to the marketplace. They survive when they deliver innovative solutions that demonstrate improved performance.

A STEP AHEAD

Those who practice reactive business respond to a client's existing perceptions and deliver services that closely match their request. These firms are a commodity. They will see revenues and profits erode as competitors that are more agile grab market share by offering lower cost or greater benefit.

However, the best-of-breed firms practice a collaborative approach that aligns with their client's business goals. Their approach anticipates the ways their services can provide advantage toward meeting those goals. They put most of their energy into positioning their firm with the type

The Architecture of Value

of client who consistently provides profitable work. They offer new services that help those clients to leverage the solution they have provided. They offer innovative services in the areas of content, connection, or control.

They work in a collaborative way with their clients—asking relevant questions, listening to their concerns, and working together with a partnering attitude. They are the essence of the word *teamwork*.

How do you become more preactive? Focus on clients who have shared complaints in the last year and address the internal processes (or people) that led to those problems. Solutions to these issues help you differentiate your services from your competitors.

Do not focus only on clients in growth sectors. Look for opportunities with potential clients whose business is down—your competitors are probably ignoring them. Get more in touch with current projects. Call your current clients and check on their perception of progress.

THE MODERN ENTERPRISE

Modern organizations—public or private—have similar overarching issues. Advanced information technology is their central concern. Today, every organization searches for profitability (or reduced costs) and a path to increased stakeholder value. They develop strategies that anticipate the impact of technology to their marketplace, to their competition, or to their internal processes.[69]

Information technology is at the center of that strategy. The ability for companies to extract relevant data and vital knowledge into information that can benefit all aspects of the operation is critical. Look for ways to use your firm's technical expertise to communicate, distribute, or deliver that important data—particularly if you have insights into the niche data of your service sector.

Teamwork

VALUE PROPOSITION

Demonstrating leadership through insight, innovation, and cohesion for the client provides long-term value and builds the trust necessary to help move projects forward. A client is more likely to advance an initiative if they believe that you share common values and that their success matters to you as much as your profitability.

Today, client service known for "over promising and under delivering" is, unfortunately, rampant. This is not specific to a particular industry and seems to transcend virtually all businesses and organizations. Changing that fundamental feature—everywhere the client has a touch point—will go a long way to cementing a long-term, recurring relationship. These points of contact exist at many levels:

- **First contact** by marketing and business development staff
- **Ongoing communication** with consultants, designers, project managers, technical staff, and field personnel
- **Back-office finance** staff handling billing and collections
- **Management and leadership** seeking to build strategic advantage

Each of these is important to communicating value.

CROSS-FUNCTIONAL DATA

One method to improve relationships is to provide tools and processes that engage and focus all aspects of your business to the services you offer to clients. The increasing complexity of sales channels and services make working together to build improved client relationships critical to everyone's success. Similarly, the inter-relationships between various disciplines require a network of relationships (between both firms and individuals) that changes and evolves constantly.

Understanding which clients are most valuable or most easily grown—and which to avoid at all cost—is a daunting task when historic data is stored in separate *silos* between finance, marketing, and operations.

The Architecture of Value

Typically, this results in valuable real-time information regarding the corporate whole being lost.

Building an accessible knowledge base of client experience, with the ability for the client and alliance partners (product manufacturers, sub-contractors, allied professionals, etc.) to provide input is the mantra of the new peer-to-peer economy.

Cathy Osborne, president of Business by Design Solutions, commented, *"Business process success comes from having a long-term big picture focus, clear strategy and objectives, an executive to champion and support the initiative, a plan with separate measurable stages, and the ability to demonstrate short term success."*[70]

APPLY THESE FACTORS. Demonstrate value. Deliver experience. You will find your firm on the way to continuing and profitable work through both fast and slow times.

CHAPTER 30 | Metrics

> *Not everything that can be counted counts,*
> *and not everything that counts can be counted.*
> Albert Einstein

HOW DO YOU KNOW when your professional practice is performing to its highest potential? Ask your clients what factors they review when reviewing their own performance. They will likely tell you, *"Measure what matters. What gets measured gets done."* Even if your firm consistently operates well, new or more agile competitors may still be a challenge. If you do not regularly measure results of your own performance, you will not be ready.

BENCHMARKING

Where do you start? What do you measure? You sense your company is improving its client service, or, conversely, have a sinking feeling sales might be cooling off. Trust your gut feelings. They are usually excellent indicators as to where you can start benchmarking.

First, get solid evidence before allocating your resources to improvement. The larger and more complicated the business, the bigger the need for benchmarking. Everyone sees the business from their own perspective. You need to be able to communicate clear, consistent health-and-status messages to your people.

Benchmarks, by necessity, have numbers associated with them. Select the areas that are important to your bottom line, but that you also have control over. Market share or stock price may have a big impact on valuation and are definitely numbers. However, they do not qualify as actionable benchmarking standards because those figures depend on too many factors.

The Architecture of Value

Actionable benchmarking standards can include the following:

- **Percent** of clients rating service as "excellent" (based on a survey)
- **Number** (or percentage) of client issues resolved within 24 hours
- **Volume** of add-service sales to existing clients
- **Volume** of repeat sales to existing clients
- **Time** from award (verbal) to start of service delivery (contract)
- **Number** (or percentage) of your employees that have industry-certification training (and passed the qualifying test)
- **Number** of new sales contacts per day (week or month)
- **Ratio** of new contacts to requests for proposal or qualification
- **Ratio** of new contacts to "closed" sales

AUTOMATIC METRICS

For those things that are unique to your segment of the service industry, you will measure different aspects of you client base and interaction processes. Use existing financial or client relationship databases or data collected by project managers, business development representatives, or account managers in your CRM system. At the end of the day, measuring has to be easy or it will not work.

The automated measurement process has two significant benefits:

- **A simple, process-based tracking mechanism** always works. You can easily spend more time measuring than the measurements are worth unless you have a standardized process.
- **An automated system** with built-in objectivity promotes fairness and efficiency. People seldom object to having a process measured by a tool.

Metrics

BENCHMARKING TOOLS

There are tools for nearly every kind of benchmarking. You can customize them for your own use or you can create your own. One valuable benchmarking tool is the client survey. Conduct them at the time of sale, at the completion of the project, or at the end of a warranty period. Do them by phone, by mail, by website, or e-mail.

The information you get from your clients based on your own questions is extremely valuable. Although not every client will take the time to fill one out, most appreciate the fact that you care about their opinion. Having a survey contact after the sale can also fill a number of other purposes. They can be post-project, ensuring you have addressed all outstanding issues or questions.

Training employees is vitally important. If you train, but do not test your employees, you lose half of the value of the effort. Successful firms test their employees on product knowledge twice yearly. Employees who do not pass are required to attend additional training and retest. An employee failing three tests moves to a non-client-service position. Utilizing industry-recognized certification programs provides value by giving an opportunity to acknowledge an employee's performance.

Other tools can include time and date entries to track items statistically though your internal processes. Similarly, automated phone systems (with caller ID tied to client databases) will keep track of call sources and time spent on hold. Services and software applications can track website activity and broken links. You can revise the factors that are useful to measure, once you have a body of data to analyze, and determine how useful the comparisons are.

SETTING ACHIEVABLE GOALS

Where do you want to be and when? Prioritize your measurements. What are the areas that are most in need of improvement—not necessarily in numbers, but that would bring the biggest results to the bottom line with the least expenditure to implement change? Refine

The Architecture of Value

that concept down into a single sentence that includes a number and a date: The what, by what measure, by whom, and by when.

Examples of goals from actionable metrics can include:

- **Percent increase** in "exceptional" ratings on client surveys

- **Percent increase** in post-sale service or support contracts within 30 days of the completion of the project

- **Percent** of all client service employees who will achieve passing scores in technical knowledge within six months of implementing or improving your technical training program

- **Percent decrease** in verbal acceptance to actual billable time on service or project X

- **Number** (or percentage) of your employees that have had industry-recognized certification training

- **Percent decrease** in caller hold times

Goals should be a stretch, but achievable. You can make a goal incremental—by breaking it up into manageable pieces—giving half credit for getting halfway there, for example. Make sure that the resources to achieve the goal are available. Collaborate with your people on what is necessary to reach that goal. As one manager put it, *"Don't tell me it can't be done. Tell me what you need to get it done."*

THE HANDSHAKE

One way to ensure that business metrics are used is to set up a formal handshake agreement between teams or departments to ensure that everyone is pulling their weight to deliver on the goal.

The business development staff cannot meet their numbers if a project takes too much time and they cannot guarantee a delivery time—or worse, have missed a delivery time! An engineering team cannot meet a

Metrics

client's schedule if the business development staff provides incomplete project data.

A written agreement for all inter-departmental processes that stipulates performance expectations, ensures a reliable and repeatable effort, and creates a measurable (and rewardable) standard. After reviewing the process and negotiating and writing agreements, your staff will have a new awareness of how their jobs contribute to the overall picture. The experience of synergy and being part of a larger whole adds to the motivation and creativity they bring to their jobs every day.

WHAT'S IN IT FOR ME?

Being able to quantify a team or department's contribution to the final product or service of your firm gives a basis for the company to evaluate incentive compensation. Bonuses based on contribution to meeting the measurements that management sets have an obvious value by rewarding the producers.

Be clear, consistent, and communicative about incentives. Bonuses awarded in public (through high-attendance meetings, newsletters, or intranet postings) have an added benefit to the individual—they get the recognition of their peers. It focuses attention on the metrics in a very material way and people start watching their numbers when they see what is in it for them.

LESSONS LEARNED

Best practices always come from the understanding that you do not always do everything perfectly the first time. After the schedule has passed for each of your goals, get the people involved together and review—in an open-forum session—what worked, and what did not. Improve future performance by identifying processes that should change. Then set the bar higher for your next project.

The Architecture of Value

BY BENCHMARKING APPROPRIATE METRICS, setting goals, measuring progress, providing incentives, and capturing lessons learned, you begin the sustainable process of continuous improvement. By constantly improving and changing your business processes and involving your entire organization, you stay flexible to market changes. Moreover, you stay ahead of the competition.

CHAPTER 31 | Opportunity

Daring ideas are like chessmen moved forward.
They may be beaten, but they may start a winning game.
Johann Wolfgang Von Goethe

HOW OFTEN HAS THIS HAPPENED TO YOU? A client seeking a consultant releases a request for qualifications or proposal for a proposed major and complex project. It sounds interesting. However, the scope of work is vague and the stated expectations are unclear.

To complicate the matter, a third-party client's representative is in charge and there is limited access to the end-users. The appropriate level of project funding seems to be questionable, but cast in stone. The project schedule is too short for adequate service, but is just long enough to permit the delusion that you can meet the overall schedule.

No standards typically used by this client will apply until after the first round of consulting is complete. The change order process is unreasonable, but characterized as a deal breaker if you try to modify it. Fee allocations seem equally unreasonable (*"We know you can do it for less."*) drawn from a history of simpler projects with lesser scope and lower budget.

REALITY SETS IN

In this age of rapid information, client expectations rarely seem to be in harmony with the reality of delivering a high-quality project. Thus, it becomes very important to ensure that your contract defines deliverables and labor (not to mention function and capability). It should be complete and inclusive of protections from the vagaries of unclear client desires.

The Architecture of Value

Contractual language in the form of direct statements of work or in an attached terms and conditions sheet can improve your firm's approach to business. Because of the variations in legal requirements on a state-by-state and local level, it is safe, if not always pleasant, to check with your attorney before finalizing any contractual change to your standards procedures.

I have listed several contract ideas that I think are highly relevant.[71] Apply them, as appropriate, to meet your own specific circumstances.

PREPAYMENT
Establish a reasonable percentage for a down payment to start the project. It should cover the immediate working capital required to begin the work. If the project has a short duration schedule, it is appropriate to request 100 percent of the fee up-front. If it will last longer, request a proportionally lesser amount.

CANCELLATION
If accepting a project prevents you from taking on other work (due to schedule conflicts or staffing limitations), include a clause that requires a cancellation fee if the work stops. This fee should be immediately due and payable on a sliding schedule; more if the project stops early (within 30 days), less as more work is completed (and billed normally). This is especially true for large projects that demand a large percentage of your overall resources.

CONTINGENCY
The purpose of contingency funds is to pay for any unanticipated changes that occur during the course of the design and construction of the project. For those unanticipated changes (to scope, schedule, or budget), insist the client budget extra funds in their initial financing.

Opportunity

It is not unusual to discover unknown conditions, schedule conflicts or extensions, or people, product, or service availability along the way that have a significant impact on the overall budget (and as a result your fees). Find the funds to cover these contingencies early. They may not be easy to secure later in the project.

INVOICING
Define the invoicing procedure according to what is easiest and best for you, as opposed to that of the client. This sets the stage for additional fees should the client want to vary from your standard.

ALTERNATIVES
Set a limit to the amount of "consulting" that goes into the project. You can set a limit on the number of alternatives you will provide under the contract. Alternatively, you can limit the hours expended. Set a completion date for your work—a point where work is considered complete— to ensure you are paid for your efforts on the project.

ESCALATION
Inflationary pressure often results in higher costs during the lifetime of a project. Include an escalation clause in your contract that specifies that after a certain date, fees and rates will increase by a set percentage, and then annually by another. While most firms put a clause in their contracts stating that after some date fees will be subject to renegotiation, this is better protection. An escalation clause helps avoid a renegotiation that could result in decreased fees.

LIABILITY
Limit any liabilities incurred during the course of a project to a maximum of the net contract amount received by your firm (not including reimbursable expenses and subcontractors) at the point when you incur the liability. This is a more reasonable limit of liability than the total fee.

The Architecture of Value

CONTRACT
Set a time limit for the client to sign your contract, as well as an end date for the contract. Do not make open-ended commitments that you may not want to live up to in the future. This clause helps define the time of the project completion.

COPYRIGHT
Because documents used for other than their original purpose may result in unforeseen liability to the original consultancy, it is important to limit the usage to the specific project they represent. Including a warning clause should prevent an unscrupulous client from trying to rubber stamp your design on future work.

REIMBURSABLES
One of the most time consuming (and money wasting) efforts in project billing is accounting for reimbursable expenses. Include a line item in each invoice for a fixed percentage of the monthly fee to cover most non-labor expense costs. Check your project histories to determine what percentage is appropriate for your firm. This type of clause greatly simplifies accounting time and saves money. It also eliminates the need to keep track of the volumes of receipts. If a client insists on copies of receipts, consider charging an administrative fee per invoice, plus $1.00 per copy of supporting data.

I AM NOT IN THE BUSINESS of rendering legal advice. However, I believe this would be their advice: *"The contract terms listed above should only be used after consultation with a competent attorney knowledgeable in contract law in your area of practice and locality."* This does not diminish the importance of solid contracts that reflect your requirements as an important part of the experience you have with your clients, and they with you. Creating healthy contracts is, in the end, another element to a successful practice and long-term viability.

CHAPTER 32 | Agreement

A verbal agreement isn't worth the paper it's written on.
Samuel Goldwyn

OVER THE COURSE OF THE PAST 40 YEARS, working on several hundred projects with project managers from all disciplines, the number one complaint I have heard is that they did not completely understand the client's expectations.

During the strategic planning phase of proposal preparation—before securing the contract—the word *"assume"* is seriously overused (followed closely by *"in my years of experience"*—which is usually the basis of the assumption). Remember, you base assumptions on *your* perceptions of the project, not necessarily those of the client.

Depending on your knowledge of specific needs, your experience (and willingness to acknowledge past failures), and the time available for and quality of your research at this critical phase of the project, you often assume you know the client—what they will do, what they will need, their important issues, their schedule, and their budget. Only after you sign the contract do you learn that some, if not all, of those assumptions were wrong.

Fortunately, the project manager is in the best position to hear what the client really wants and can share with the client what you know and how you approach each project's implementation. By communicating this information early, the project manager ensures better understanding of the appropriate deliverables by knowing what the client really wants to have done. Beyond *"a quality project, on time, and on budget,"* a clear definition of function, performance, and cost alleviates subjective opinions for project satisfaction.

The Architecture of Value

MAKE A LIST, CHECK IT TWICE

It is important to discuss these issues early, openly, and prior to completing the proposal, project plan, and contractual obligations. These become the basis for the agreement to perform the work. To this end, the project manager should make a list of the major assumptions about the project, and then review them with the client. Developing a mutual agreement of scope, schedule, personnel, and costs will save time and money later. At this point, draft an appropriate proposal.

The contract should also include the caveat that if any of the assumptions on which you based the agreements change, you will put the project on *hold* until you reach a new agreement. As an example, if the client's representative changes, your action will be to stop work until the new representative acknowledges and accepts the performance criteria established (or accepts the increase in your fees for changes to the contract and terms).

Controlling your own destiny is to empower your project manager's with an understanding of the importance of each project to the success of your business. The following ten important rules of professional practice[72] should set the approach for each project:

1. **Profit:** We are in the business to make money, or we will not grow or survive.
2. **Non-Profit**: Like any rule, there are exceptions. Review the reasons for taking a non-profitable (or pro bono) project in the context of the long-term goals with that particular client relationship.
3. **Budget:** Prepare a project budget tied to a well-defined scope of work. More definition is better, particularly tied to schedule expectations.
4. **Change:** Do not change the scope of work without a corresponding change in schedule and/or fee. As noted above, a

Agreement

contract and work plan that carefully defines expectations is much easier to adjust with full client agreement.

5. **Authorization**: Never begin work without a signed contract. At a minimum, send a letter of understanding, if you must start billable time before receiving the client's formal approval. Proper and formal authorization is a legal protection of your company's interests.

6. **Invoice**: Set a firm schedule for submitting bills for all accumulated time and reimbursable expenses. The little, innocuous things add up. Watch blueprint charges, express mail bills, travel, and per diem—all easily collectable, but you have to remember to send a bill.

7. **Collect**: Avoid new work from any client who has not paid their bill. Hey, we are not here to finance our clients; see rule number 1.

8. **Stop**: You should not continue to work on a project for a client who has not paid a bill. Deadbeats beware! Establish an accounts receivable system that closely monitors payment progress and do not be afraid to protect your own interest with a stop-work clause.

9. **Document**: Be thorough. Keep a record of everything. Meeting notes, phone conversations, submittal logs, etc., should all be part of the project file. From schedules to labor estimates, the more detail in the project record, the better. You never know when you will need it.

10. **Communicate**: It all comes back to follow-up and follow-through. Call early when you are going to be late. Ask questions when you do not know. Respond quickly and thoroughly.

The Architecture of Value

THE KEYS TO SUCCESS

Building a strong understanding of client expectations includes several important elements.

- **Recognize** the nature of the relationship. Treat the client as a person, rather than a representative of an agency or organization. Working on a personal level builds trust.

- **Strive** to see the project from the client's interests. A client once told me that he truly valued our services when he walked into a meeting and could not distinguish between his staff and ours—we acted as if we worked *for* his company, not as an outside consultant.

- **Practice** honesty, straightforward actions, and respect. Be on time, be efficient, present both sides of a situation for each recommendation, admit when you do not know, acknowledge mistakes (and suggest corrective measures), and pay attention to details.

IF YOU FOLLOW THESE SIMPLE RULES you will reach healthy and mutually satisfactory contractual agreements, provide the kind of experience that will engender the loyalty from your clients, and become the envy of your competition.

CHAPTER 33 | Negotiation

It is the poor presentation of change that people resist, not change itself.
Eliyahu Goldratt

ONE OF THE DIFFICULT ASPECTS of any project is the negotiation that occurs when there are changes in scope. You strive to develop clear and mutually agreed upon goals for your projects. Inevitably, new and unforeseen developments demand adjustment to those agreements. Regardless of your consulting role, it is important to maintain a clear understanding that change happens.

It is equally important to ensure that your project staff is empowered with the processes to defend your business interests when negotiating modifications to existing contracts. Admitting and correcting mistakes is one thing. Protecting and maintaining your business' profitability from unforeseen revisions to agreed-upon scope is something else.

ACKNOWLEDGE CHANGE

One of the best ways to create a win-win scenario for change orders is to acknowledge them at the beginning of the project. Every project goes through changes and a good contract will include a change clause. This clause gives the client the right to alter the scope of work within the original contract. Done right, it provides for the business interests of both parties.

It commits the service provider to perform the extra work—while at the same time allowing you to receive extra compensation under agreed-upon procedures. The change clause provides the means by which you can incorporate suggestions for improvements to the project. This provides a method for you to claim additional compensation to cover extra work done at the direction of the client.

The Architecture of Value

TIME IS ON YOUR SIDE
Resistance to change is universal. This applies to any change, whether a multi-million-dollar problem or deciding to revise a simple choice. Client representatives need time to rationalize change and to justify the change within their organization.

Allow adequate time for the client to consider the proposed change. This gives them time to rationalize and develop reasons for acceptance of your proposal. Unresolved issues cause tension. This tension can grow into stress unless the change is resolved.

It is usually easier for clients to accept a less than ideal proposal than develop terms that are better for them. However, there should also be a time limit set on the decision process, to ensure that change is resolved within a reasonable period.

Addressing change early is equally important. Allowing unresolved contract changes to have an impact on other aspects of the project could be deadly. It is easier to negotiate as soon as you identify a potential change. This allows more alternatives and shows a willing and honest, team-oriented spirit to the client.

THE LEVEL'S IN THE DETAILS
Presenting alternatives is a proven way of directing a client to your preferred resolution of an issue. People do not like to have only one choice. More important, when backed into a no-compromise situation, most people will react by attacking your proposal.

Maintaining a strategic advantage can include presentation of similar but less desirable (from the client's perspective) alternatives. Even the semblance of choice can leave a client with the feeling that they reached the right decision even when it may be in your favor. Maintaining a strong position does not mean presenting every choice. Avoid alternatives that are less desirable from your position.

Negotiation

A client will accept a large number of small change items better than a small number of large ones. If the change is a large one, look for ways to break it down into component parts. A number of individual items with small prices are easier to discuss. They can be more readily demonstrated and tend not to create as much friction as one large cost issue. When presented with a breakdown, clients can more easily understand the value of the change request.

AVOIDING BOILERPLATE

Many consultant-driven reports would easily be one-third their size if it were not for boilerplate. They use these collections of long-winded, cryptic, and confusing clauses to catch everything that falls through the cracks of their advice. This tactic is effective for the client (and the consultant) if the integrator uses it to deny or disavow a rightful change of scope.

Good consultants know how to describe their intent for function, performance, and conformance. This allows responsible integrators to understand the project's requirements and price the project properly. By contrast, boilerplate used in an effort to cover the lazy consultant's errors and omissions usually fails to address specific situations.

When a consultant uses boilerplate, it can become the source of requests for information or clarification (ultimately leading to change orders). Avoiding meaningless, catchall phraseology improves the collaboration between consultant, client, and integrator, and reduces unnecessary costs and changes.

The Architecture of Value

TRY TO SEE BOTH SIDES. Before developing any negotiation strategy, try to put yourself in the client's place. Look at the situation from their viewpoint. Ask what decisions are important, and why they have not already made them. Ask yourself what action you can take that would make it easier for them to reach a decision. Allowing empathy for both your client's and your positions will strengthen your ability to provide a mutually satisfying experience.

CHAPTER 34 | Dialogue

A great truth is a truth whose opposite is also a great truth.
Thomas Mann

ONE OF THE MOST COMMON and most dreaded experiences in any business day is *the meeting*. At worst, meetings can be time wasting, stifling, boring, and confrontational. At best, a well-planned and well-run meeting can be the site of true collaborative dialogue and the center of communication that furthers the goals of your business. Unfortunately, the former tends to be the norm. However, that does not mean you cannot change your approach and develop processes that improve this everyday necessity.

Marketing consultant, Kay Godwin, suggests, *"The team meeting needs to provide a safe place where self-doubts can be expressed and solutions can be found. If we recognize that failure to accomplish a task is a sign of discomfort rather than unwillingness, we can find solutions, encourage each other, and celebrate every step made toward the larger goals."*

A CLEAR APPROACH

Harvey Mackay, business consultant and author, set out eight key ingredients to a productive meeting.[73]

- **Have an agenda.** Make it detailed, time specific, and goal oriented. In addition, most importantly, distribute it to the participants before the meeting, so they come prepared

- **Stick to the time allotted.** Start on time and end on time. Keep the discussion on topic. If there are issues that are not covered, or discussions that need to be continued, set up separate schedules for those to be completed

- **Limit interruptions.** That means no cell phones, no in-house emergencies (unless it is a client), and no coffee breaks (be prepared)

- **Only invite necessary participants.** This ensures that those involved can (and will) contribute to the goal of the meeting

- **Encourage creativity.** Using allotted discussion time for brainstorming (no wrong answers or bad ideas here) can keep meetings interesting and bring out new concepts and approaches to old problems. For recurring meetings, revolve the meeting's moderator. Sometimes a fresh face generates a fresh perspective

- **Consider the location.** Does the meeting need to happen in the same conference room every time? Is there a more appropriate place to address a particular issue (like a client's site)? Is there a location more conducive to creative thinking (outdoors)?

- **Create an action plan.** Ensure that participants have clear expectations and timelines for returning deliverables (what, by whom, and by when). Progress is measurable only when there is something to measure

- **End with a synopsis of the assignments.** Document deadlines and, most important, acknowledge the accomplishments. This final touch improves morale and demonstrates that a good meeting has value to the participants and the company

GROUND RULES

Peter Nosler, former CEO of DPR Construction, an innovative design/build-oriented general contractor, set out twelve similar ground rules for every meeting.[74] The list is illustrative of DPR's creative approach and are posted on the wall of every conference room and construction site:

1. This is a safe zone
2. No rank in the room
3. Everyone participates; no one dominates
4. Help us stay on track

Dialogue

5. Focus on the process
6. Listen as an ally
7. One speaker at a time
8. Be an active listener
9. Give freely of your experience
10. Actively agree, but only if it makes sense to you
11. Correctly spell anything you write on a flip chart
12. Encourage having fun

At the conclusion of each meeting, Nosler suggests that the group have a "plus/delta" discussion that highlights what worked and what did not (and the changes necessary to correct them in the future), as a way to encourage continual improvement of the process. This lessons learned approach works equally well as a "lessons learned" meeting at the end of projects, and has become a popular tool for those practicing the Lean Six-Sigma process-oriented management programs.[***]

MAKING MEETINGS WORK

There are problems common to many meetings, including *the multi-headed animal syndrome*—where everyone is working on a different agenda. As a result, there are unintended outcomes. There is often confusion between process and content; the difference between how you discuss or approach a topic versus what you are discussing.

[***] "Lean" and "Six Sigma" are complementary management processes. If performed properly, they represent a long-term business initiative that can produce unprecedented results. Lean makes sure you are *working on the right activities*, and Six Sigma makes sure *you are doing the right things right* the very first time we do them. Lean defines and establishes the value flow as pulled by the client, and Six Sigma makes the value flow smoothly without interruption.

The Architecture of Value

Personal attacks can be debilitating to the meeting process. Watch out for hidden agendas.

Discussion bottlenecks occur when the group leader does not monitor the flow of information. When roles and responsibilities are unclear, people do not know what is expected. When the group leader uses the meeting as a personal forum, collaboration goes out the window. Another problem is data overload. If you address too many issues, but you do not allot enough time, nothing can be resolved.

Repetition and wheel spinning is a common problem in regularly scheduled meetings. When you cover the same ground repeatedly, there will be no apparent action. If the leader approaches every decision with a win/lose attitude, polarization and low commitment is common. Similarly, confused objectives and expectations create unnecessary delays in reaching consensus. If the issues of power and authority are not clear (*"Can you make this decision?"*), action is difficult to take.

Denial of problems is an all too common issue. The status quo is the easy path, but often leads to stagnation. This can result in negative attitudes and avoidance of challenge. Communication problems result from individuals not being involved and not listening.

The environment (as we in the building industry know all too well) can play an important role. If participants cannot hear, cannot see, or are too hot or too cold, it is difficult to conduct a productive discussion. Lack of openness and trust fosters tensions that can undermine even the most important meeting. Leadership *must* address these issues.

The key to the success of any meeting is planning and preparation. As noted previously, address objectives and expectations, meeting type, group composition, size, involvement and participation, room arrangement, individual responsibilities, and authority before any meeting happens.

Dialogue

The methods and techniques for the discussion, agenda, presentation format, record, and summary of desired outcome, tasks, deadlines, and responsibilities are the key factors to a successful meeting. Consider using an interaction method—that consists of four key participants—to make any meeting work better· the interactive roles are:

- **Facilitator:** A neutral member of the group, whose task is to keep the meeting on topic and ensure everyone participates; the facilitator has the responsibility for the logistics of the meeting (input on agenda, schedule, and support)

- **Recorder:** Also neutral and serves as a scribe of the important issues discussed; annotate notes on flip charts and post around the room to foster improved group memory

- **Member:** The individual participant takes an active role in the discussion

- **Chair:** The one with final decision-making power, but who otherwise acts and interacts like any other group member

With this facilitated, documented, and time-monitored approach, even a simple meeting can have better results.[75]

YOU CANNOT AVOID MEETINGS. We are a society where small groups meet to collaborate, to share, to solve problems, and to set direction for your organization's growth. Studies indicate that members of management tend to spend 35 to 50 percent of their time in meetings. Discovering and practicing methods to improve the quality and value of these group interactions can save money, increase productivity, and contribute to an improved bottom line. Look for ways to make your meetings a better experience. It will pay off.

The Architecture of Value

CHAPTER 35 | Communication

If you do not like the laws of physics, invent one of your own.
Anonymous

ONE OF THE CHALLENGES faced by both the contractor and the design consultant in the consumer and commercial market place is meeting the expectations of clients who have strongly held beliefs in one or more critical aspects of the project.

This can span project concept, schedule, component selection, or performance. The intricacies of architecture, engineering, and construction fall in that gray area of client knowledge where you are more than likely to meet someone holding a dogmatic perspective—a rigidly held opinion or belief—that is in direct conflict with your perception of reality. Unfortunately, unless you take precautions, their reality usually overrules.

GREAT (BUT HIGHLY UNREALISTIC) EXPECTATIONS

When the project first starts, you are in a phase analogous to the honeymoon. Everyone is happy. The simple decision to hire you (the expert) establishes your credibility. No one wants to rock the proverbial boat (yet). Your first series of meetings allows *blue-sky* project concepts to be developed. There are no constraints on your vision for the perfect solution to their project's challenge. Important issues, which will rise up later, seem trivial.

Existing data, new criteria, or the simple physics of some soon-to-be-released, new technology do not compromise the project design ideal. The client's vision or factors outside of your control do not affect your idea for the technical solution.

The Architecture of Value

Even without the input or impact of users that you have not yet met, you know operational functionality will be very intuitive. Budget is not an issue even worth discussing; the benefit from this implementation will clearly improve overall (pick one)—productivity, effective communication, teamwork, or impact. *("After all, how much could it possibly cost?")*

It becomes imperative to go on record early—and sometimes often—before things start to get out of hand. Honesty is still the best policy. Setting expectations early, based on clear, accurate, functional specifications and cost models, will simplify the task of proof-of-performance later.

YOU WANT IT WHEN?

You are often at the mercy of schedule changes outside of your control. Sometimes client representatives put a low priority on a particular requirement and do not raise it as a program issue until the project has completed. On the other hand, the prime consultant fails to provide the other sub-consultants with information in a timely manner or coordinate the work, causing sub-consultants to re-design.

A consultant may specify a critical component *("no substitutions")* that cannot be delivered by the manufacturer within the timeframe of the project. Alternatively, the integrator or one of their subs does not finish work as promised, ahead of the final project due date, delaying the completion of your work.

The schedule for everything—from the first set of planning documents to the last set of post project analyses—poses a logistic factor, which will affect your success. More than likely, unless you only work on one project at a time, conflicting schedules of multiple projects will cause your hair to gray (or fall out) before you learn the *magic* of the balance between want and need.

Communication

Again, communication can come to your rescue. Never, in the spirit of teamwork, be afraid to flag the critical milestones to your implementation. Nor is it inappropriate to raise them again, if they continue to have a negative impact on your performance.

TECHNOLOGY FOR TECHNOLOGISTS

Technology selection is usually a matter of *"the best bang for the buck"* to meet a certain technical objective—unless, of course, your client (or his boss, brother-in-law, or best friend) has just heard about (or seen on PBS' Nova) some new wonder widget that would be perfect (and now required) for his project.

More challenging still is the client who found a deal at the local consumer home improvement center and is certain that it will be just perfect for their project. In the worst case, the latest promise of *"digitally-processed, hyper-performance, space-age alloy-construction"* enamors your designer or a recent promotional contest (known in sales jargon as a *spiff*) on some loss leader product unduly influences your account manager.

In the end, you (and your client) are better off when you provide a reasonable set of alternatives (at least two, three is better) for performance and price. If it means revealing flaws in some, so be it. Clients are sometimes misinformed, but rarely are they completely oblivious to the options of anything costing in excess of their perception of value.

Better to offer credible analysis along with your commitment to service and support for the final choice, rather than to try to slip in a lesser-performing solution and risk losing the relationship completely.

The Architecture of Value

MIND OVER MUDDLE

Most architects will acknowledge that their clients generally have a difficult time visualizing how their new building or space will look from viewing a set of two-dimensional plans. Similarly, clients rarely read written descriptions. Project details, diagrams (no matter how cleverly illustrated), and itemized budgets usually do not convey the reality of the finished project, which remains only a perception to the client.

In architecture, with the advent of building information modeling (3-dimensional fly-through software), this challenge has been somewhat mitigated. Though the technology is expensive and time-consuming, it is worth the cost and effort when it prevents *"that's not what I thought it would look like."*

For any other service, hands-on demonstrations or views of similar projects (especially if that client is a positive reference for you) are still the best way to show the functionality and impact of a particularly esoteric application. Virtual solutions are getting better, but still have a long way to go before they really reflect reality.

CLOSING THE GAP

In the end, the project's complete (you think) and, surprise, the client says it is not what they wanted or expected, does not work (right) or someone (not involved in any of the planning) says the same thing, but carries higher authority within the client's organization.

You react, trying not to be defensive, pointing out the specific (recorded) choices the client made during the process that led to the result. The client responds, *"It doesn't matter!"* The client is always right. This is why relationships are important. A strong relationship can mitigate this type of conflict.

Communication

EFFECTIVE COMMUNICATION REMAINS an often-elusive goal for the service industry professional. The art of active listening—restating what you have heard and adding your analysis—is critical. Conveying concepts and recommendations and maintaining the spirit of problem solving that engaged you in the first place are all important. Remembering, *"the client is always right"* does not mean you cannot help them be right in their decisions. In the end, the client will remember you (and the project) by the quality of the communication.

The Architecture of Value

CHAPTER 36 | Challenge

The greatest challenge to any thinker is stating the problem in a way that will allow a solution.
Bertrand Russell

EVERY PROJECT BEGINS WITH A VISION of an ideal outcome—a cool solution, seamless integration of state-of-the-art technology, and improved communications for the client—all provided on time and on budget.

Unfortunately, as a project manager, you stumble across the occasional land mine. This may occur because of unstated or unclear goals for the scope of the project, changes in the budget, or revisions to the schedule.

When you combine complex issues and high expectations for results with a new implementation, reality is often different from perception. Approaching inevitable challenges, developing lasting solutions, and communicating the process with your clients creates better outcomes.

As an effective project manager, you need to overcome these challenges. Remember the three Cs of effective project management: *clarity*, *collaboration*, and *communication*. They are easy to say, but harder to do. However, by exploring these concepts through real-world stories, you will see how it is possible to overcome these challenges.

Just as every project has an ideal vision, every project also has key elements that nearly always determine its success or failure. These factors are scope, schedule, and budget. Manage these elements effectively and your project will succeed. Lose control of them and your project is doomed for failure. Remember these elements. They should probably be your mantra. They are definitely your responsibility.

A fourth element is just as vital and transcends the other three factors: people. People can make or break a project. You work internally with management, sales and marketing, designers, consultants, and technicians and externally with the client's project manager, executives,

The Architecture of Value

user groups, and a wide array of other stakeholders and service providers. The result will be as influenced by each part as by the sum of the whole.

The human element is always volatile. Therefore, people are often the root cause for most of the project manager's challenges. This people element can be overwhelming and is probably worthy of another chapter. For now, I will focus on the first three key issues and intertwine the fourth in addressing some solutions.

SOME DEFINITIONS

Projects commonly go through six distinct phases. At each phase, more information is gathered, more influences (and influencers) become part of the mix, and the project manager's responsibilities for input, deliverables, and logistics is more critical. Similarly, the project manager must coordinate those whose actions affect these responsibilities.

The following descriptions of the six phases of a project provide context for a typical project. Sometimes the client will chose an alternative project delivery method to compress the first three phases of design. This allows earlier determination of a guaranteed maximum price (GMP) to be established and accepted. The integrator executes the final three phases of responsibilities:

1. **Feasibility:** These elements are the foundation of project's program development. At this phase, you define specific areas of the scope: environmental (what impact will it have?), spatial (how big is it?), functional (what does it do?), and technical (what systems do they need?). Identify, catalog, and summarize global issues. Establish the budget on an order-of-magnitude-of-importance basis. The project manager's responsibility is to ensure that proper input is gathered and design concepts are consistent with good practice. Reference costs estimates to similar work.

Challenge

2. **Concept:** As the first representation of the project, this phase defines important issues and begins to develop the envelope (the basis of design). Identify budgets on a granular level referenced to recent experience on similar projects. The project manager accounts for the support systems needed to meet the technical requirements.

3. **Design:** This phase takes the schematic concept into the multiple dimensions of space, time, and cost. Detail elements are developed. Identify and share expectations with the other members of the team for interconnectivity and synergy with other systems. Budgets are specific, mostly at a generic, component level and labor-cost basis. At this phase, budgets are set in stone. The project manager must be wary of changes.

4. **Documentation:** Detailed analysis, drawings, and specifications define what responsibilities the integrator will have. Very specific details of technical inter-relationships and integration are set forth and they are both illustrated and specified. The document package represents the responsibilities of the integrator, as defined by the designer.

    This should be a *red flag* moment as it is often the basis for litigation after the project is complete and based on someone else's interpretation and execution. Base the budget on manufacturer/model number-specific choices. This makes change more difficult.

5. **Negotiations:** In most of the world, this phase is where low bid wins. In the alternative compressed-schedule scenario, this step establishes a GMP, and takes place before the construction documents are prepared. In either case, it sets the client's expectation for the delivery of the finished project, both in cost and schedule. It is the time that the project manager—either consultant or integrator—has many a sleepless night thinking, *"What did I forget?"*

The Architecture of Value

6. **Administration:** This is the "build" part of the project. For the designer, it includes the submittal review, coordination with field installation, testing, and acceptance. For the integrator, it encompasses engineering, procurement, infrastructure confirmation, and systems integration and testing. Raise missed or forgotten items in this phase. Change orders appear—an embarrassment for the designer or the integrator—and a negotiation challenge for the client.

Regardless of the delivery method, challenges faced by the project manager remain constant. Yet understanding each phase and addressing the relevant issues is critical to your ultimate success, as is managing the three elements of scope, schedule and budget.

THE SCOPE

Why are we here? Defining the scope of services is the first step to a successful project. Identifying (and meeting) the client's goals and determining how success is measured will inevitably lead to a satisfied client and potentially, repeat business. What does the client want, need, or expect? Answers are sometimes confusing and hard to come by.

The source of confusion often begins with the initial request for proposal. Projects have many layers of input. For instance, the client's user group defines a need. The client's operations staff catalogs the needs and prepares a request for proposal. In many cases, they release it to a select set of consultants. They, in turn, solicit input from other consulting firms, if the scope includes needs outside of their core competency. If this sounds a bit like the childhood game of telephone—it is. With so many voices in the mix, it is not surprising that the initial request bears little resemblance to the request for proposal.

Unfortunately, the program defined by the user (and translated by the client's program manager and then interpreted by the consultant) is usually not very specific about expectations or needs. Hence, danger

Challenge

looms when the consulting firm moves ahead with the project without the input from other, necessary professionals.

Additionally, the client establishes the budget for the project to benchmark responses against a pre-established cost goal. That is good if the client has a recent project to compare to, but often the budget is set against a prior implementation that may be too old (or too different) to be relevant. Over this amount of time, not only has the solution changed, but the cost of the project and labor has changed—and not for the better.

Scope has always been hard to pin down. No matter how experienced a client is with the issue, they base decisions on one set of perspectives that change as the client's organization changes. A client can agree to a detailed scope, only to have it modified as internal responsibilities shift within the client organization. A new person brought in late usually brings a new and different perspective, and may have experiences, opinions, and prejudices that alter the project definition.

Further, clients often lack technical expertise and make decisions based on input from internal sources not directly responsible for the project.

PERSPECTIVE

I had an experience as a consultant to a Silicon Valley start-up. The client had based a technical decision on internal input instead of taking my advice. On completion (and with underwhelming results), the client's manager asked me, *"Why didn't you tell me I was being stupid?"* It did not matter that I *had* given the right advice (in writing), but from their perspective I was not strong enough in the delivery of my advice. As the project manager, I took the fall, making restitution to a new solution my responsibility.

The Architecture of Value

What should you do in this situation? *Document! Document! Document!* Keep a very open and regular dialogue on potential changes and the impact of change decisions. What advice (arguments) did you make to your client in writing? Make your position clear, early, and repeated with each change. Start the documentation process from day one. Strength of conviction and commitment to clarity are important lessons from those who have learned the hard way.

THE SCHEDULE

Who's on first? Why is the technology integrator always the last man standing? In the systems world, the confusion usually stems from not understanding technology and its impact on the organization. Unfortunately (and too often,) it is the last element considered by the client's management team. Due to typical logistics, it's also the last system installed in a larger implementation. As a result, the project manager is continually playing catch up with a team that is already down the road.

PERSPECTIVE

"Why didn't I call you sooner?" was heard from the facilities director of a charitable foundation when he realized that neither he nor his architect had given any thought to technology until the project was at the building-permit stage (the end of the construction document phase). At this phase, every input from a designer or integrator would cause delays and increased cost.

Management would need to review and approve any changes to the budget (which was nonexistent). Moreover, they thought they had a fixed price for their project. Fortunately, the general contractor was able to adjust the schedule to allow for the new input, and the integrator's price was absorbed by the *contingency* built into the overall budget.

Challenge

Before submitting your proposal, schedule expectations and your ability to meet them should be the reviewed with your business developer. Expectations for delivery, based on mistaken or overlooked criteria, are often the root cause of problems. Again, the problem is yours, notwithstanding your client's delay in realizing their need for your support.

Further complicating the issue, the digital age has brought about the perception that expected results should be instantaneous. As a Wall Street broker once asked me, *"What do you mean I can't have it tomorrow?"* His multi-million dollar deals were made on the spot, so why the technology could not be installed immediately. It did not matter that we had not designed anything or started the procurement process.

Learning the lesson of time management could mean saying *"no."* Sometimes it means you will turn down the project. Before you commit to a negative response, remember to temper your question with *"when?"* This could mean the difference between turning down a project and negotiating a successful solution. Propose a realistic schedule that meets the client's beneficial use needs—aligned with the abilities of you, your suppliers, and other key contributors. This is the path to achievement. In the end, clients forget schedule issues first, if the project is a technical success.

THE BUDGET

What does it cost? This question is usually the last one asked and the first questioned. As with scheduling, the source of confusion often comes from pre-feasibility studies—when the client internally establishes a budget based on their last somewhat-similar project. The pitfalls are the same: too long ago to remember and not incremented for inflation or technological advancement. I recall a facility manager for an internet company, perplexed about how to pay for their budget, asking *"But what if we don't have a million dollars?"* They had budgeted

The Architecture of Value

only $300K for a $1.2M wish list. For a multi-national organization, I thought they would have known better.

Not all is lost. Phasing project implementation is a good way to address this challenge. Alternately, because change is a constant, finding *"responsible minimum investment"* solutions to meeting their needs will endear you to your clients. They will appreciate that you did not gold plate your proposal with unneeded expenses or untried ideas. Again, clearly document the proposal in user-friendly, easy-to-understand terminology. Most importantly, provide an accurate cost estimate to avoid this project manager's dilemma.

MANY HAVE WRITTEN ABOUT EFFECTIVE PROJECT MANAGEMENT. However, at the end of the day and after 40 years of practice, I believe effective project management boils down to the three Cs: clarity, collaboration, and communication. Keep these principles foremost in your mind and apply them to all that you do. Remember, almost everyone has the same ideal for the project's outcome, and working together, it is achievable.

CHAPTER 37 | Evolution

All progress is initiated by challenging current conceptions; and executed by supplanting existing institutions.
George Bernard Shaw

ONE POSITIVE TREND in the building industry is the extension of experience-driven, qualifications-based selection (QBS) to all members of the team.††† While the request for proposal (RFP) will still be used for many sub-consultants and sub-contractors on many projects (i.e., low price wins), cost-based bidding seems to be diminishing in popularity and effectiveness. It is important that you learn to educate your clients on the benefits of making a credentials-based choice.

Today, the best clients to work with are those clients who want the most qualified project delivery team to do the work. They are not seeking the consultant who only meets the basic qualifications for the project or the integrator with the lowest bid. Basic qualifications rarely bring *vision* to the project, and lowest cost rarely takes into account the goals the stakeholders have for a successful implementation.

Another factor changing the low-bid mentality is the importance of time. There is the time it takes to complete the project to meet the client's expectations and to be effective for the end user. In addition, there is the nuisance factor caused by the participants in an adversarial process (unneeded change orders, claims, and litigation). These factors add to the cost required by the client. They are also often beyond their expectation for involvement.

---

††† In 1972, Congress passed the Brooks Act, requiring the Federal Government to select and negotiate contracts for professional services based on demonstrated competence and qualification for the type of services required and at fair and reasonable prices. This applies to all Federal-sponsored projects. The practice extends to both public- and privately-funded projects.

The Architecture of Value

The best clients today seek a project delivery system that meets their objectives and allows for productive use of the implementation at the appointed time (or earlier) at (or better than) expected costs.

The value added brought by service and support after project completion is the one that is preferred. This productive-use factor is where the client gets the most benefit from the process. This benefit usually far outweighs the differential in design costs between the highest and lowest bidder.

DEFINING THE FUTURE

I have come to believe that the best opportunities in the future will come from responsible, collaborative strategies that work in concert with the goals of each client's project initiatives. There has long been a heated debate between pure consultants who preach clarity of intent and lack of bias and the integrators who argue that their services also encompasses design while selling and installing materials.

The reality is that you, whether consultant or contractor, provide consultative services at some level. You must provide the educational opportunities necessary to support those services at the highest and best level and promote the advantages that occur when you meet these high standards.

ACCOUNTABILITY

The only way to provide true service to your clients—the buyers of your services—is to deliver accountability and responsibility. These can only come from a practice that not only provides expertise, but also is there during and after the project completion, with total support for the client's new environment.

The only way to realize this level of accountability is to form a collaborative effort. To ignore the issue is surely the road of the past. Collaboration is the trend of the future. The importance of quality client

Evolution

service, project-focused teamwork, and professional development, which leads to creative and well-received solutions from your firm's efforts, cannot be underestimated.

NEW ROLES

We have come a long way from the architect as master builder, the supporting team as mere consultants, and the builder as just a contractor. Like any evolutionary change, there are holdovers to the traditions of the past. Today, collaboration and alliances are inevitable. The transition is challenging, the rewards untold. The challenge is for each of us as individuals to act in a collaborative manner.

Fast Company columnist Kate Kane noted, *"The job of the future is all about hyphenates—smart people who combine education, interests, and skills to become virtual one-person cross-functional teams."* She went on to say, *"The world is no longer divided into specialists who know everything about something and generalists who know something about everything."*[76]

Developing a practice model that offers both incentives for personal performance and rewards for advancing the firm's goals for growth is equally important. If you, as a professional service practitioner, are to develop an advantage, it will depend on your ability to combine (and re-combine) your knowledge and skills creatively.

WHEN YOU ASSEMBLE PROJECT TEAMS within a firm, or across multiple offices and multiple firms, made up of multi-talented people, you have the real potential for a positive experience. Evolutionary change is exciting, sometimes nerve-wracking, and always necessary to growth. It is the challenge for the *expert* who values *excellence* and delivers *experience* to their clients.

The Architecture of Value

CHAPTER 38 | Wisdom

If you are going through Hell, keep going.
Sir Winston Churchill

THE TRADITIONAL SIX PHASES OF THE PROJECT PROCESS—*feasibility, concept, design, documentation, negotiations, and administration*—cover project development from concept through completion for most professional service efforts. While this progression usually defines all the aspects of a project, it misses an important perspective.

In the real world, nothing related to a project ever ends the way it seems that it will at the start. The experiences of those involved, whether in a small effort or in a major undertaking, were first identified in the German magazine, *Der Spiegel* in December 1973, and have reappeared on the walls of design offices and construction sites—and I'm sure other professional service offices as well—ever since. Unfortunately and too often, these are the *real* phases of a project experienced by everyone during the process from start to end.

PHASE I – ENTHUSIASM
You're stoked! All the sweat and effort that have characterized the expertise and excellence of your firm's past work, that are clearly evident in your portfolio of experience, combined with the firm's marketing and the quality of your proposal and presentation, have finally landed that project of a lifetime.

This feeling of euphoria seems to transcend the relative merit, value, or importance of the job and applies as equally to that little remodel as it does to that multi-million dollar cultural icon in the city near you. It transcends the building industry and seems to be a characteristic of every team endeavor regardless of business or organizational objective.

The Architecture of Value

You share this high with all those *comrades* who will be your teammates for the next few weeks (or months or years—depending on the scale of the exercise) regardless of their discipline or responsibilities for the project's outcome. The vision of the designer, the practicality of the manager, and the efficiencies of the various supporting disciplines, all pale before the overwhelming joy of working together toward the common goal to meeting the client's needs and improving their (pick one): effectiveness, profitability, communication, etc., etc.

You begin the work with the belief that this could really be a great project—one that you will all be proud with which to be associated and one that will further your reputation and that of your peers.

PHASE II – DISILLUSIONMENT
You're bored! There does not seem to be enough time, money, or interest to provide the service you initially envisioned. An unrealistic and uncompromising budget or schedule compromised that early vision. The *state-of-the-art* is—because of something called *value engineering*—now a *state-of-the-cheap* solution. No one seems to care for your *cool* ideas, in light of many other more pressing and important issues, like the right color for the Italian marble flooring in the lobby. (Moreover, they get a trip to Italy to research it.)

Compounding your efforts are the conflicting tasks, schedules, and demands of all those other clients that are necessary to pay the rent every month. Your comrades have not lived up to your expectations. They are stubborn, silly, or stupid (from your perspective—but also note; you are equally stubborn, silly, or stupid from theirs.).

Your boss, partners, colleagues, and associates are questioning the value-to-effort ratio you pitched at the beginning of the job. Your finance department is getting increasingly noisy regarding your ability to complete the project on budget. Your internal team does not seem to share what is left of your waning enthusiasm.

PHASE III – PANIC

You're in trouble! You forgot something. Your project manager under-stated or over-stated the budget. (The former caused the client to buy that Italian marble flooring he really wanted, but now has to settle for vinyl tile; or the latter caused the client to feel he could not afford to buy that Italian marble flooring, and had to settle for vinyl tile—you get the picture.)

You thought for sure that other consultant was going to pick up those special requirements—that you all talked about in seemingly endless meetings—in their part of the work. Now the integrator is complaining that he did not include that stuff in his bid and this will cause (pick one or more): a significant delay, a significant cost increase, or a significant and costly lawsuit.

Maybe worse, the client's representative has changed and the person who set the original vision is gone and a new person with a diametrically opposed vision is saying, *"That's not what we want, need, or can afford. Please redesign, re-engineer, rebuild, etc., until it meets all of my expectations. And, we want it now! (But, remember, those all might change again tomorrow!)"*

PHASE IV – SEARCH FOR THE GUILTY

You're in hiding! This is where there actually may be some good news, because the same negative, project-related scenarios are playing out in every discipline. If you just keep your head down, you might actually escape without too much damage. The client is on a rampage. Cost overruns, schedule extensions, and threats of litigation from disgruntled contractors and suppliers all seem to have converged on the same place at the same time. Senior management is threatening to bring in a new team to finish the job *"if you guys can't get your s**t together, now!"*

The Architecture of Value

The responsible project manager revisits each decision that got you all here. The client hires outside experts for advice, counsel, and coerce action. Subtle, or sometimes more overt, efforts pin accountability on some aspect of the process that will save the time, money, or image of the original project. If you are lucky, your firm's niche is trivial in comparison to some larger flaw.

PHASE V – PUNISHMENT OF THE INNOCENT
You're toast! Unfortunately, the residue from the proverbial fan tends to land on the least responsible party. More often than not, it is a sub-contractor who did not meet schedule (usually due to factors outside of their control, i.e., the failure of other trades to meet theirs) or one that could not execute a notional concept masquerading as a specification prepared by a semi-qualified consultant.

If the uproar over finding a culprit is loud enough, it is usually enough of a distraction to allow the rest of the team to complete their work without too much further ado. If the axe falls on the client's side, the blame usually on the most vocal *visionary* for having the misplaced idea in the first place.

PHASE VI – PRAISE & HONOR FOR THE NON-PARTICIPANTS
You're history! The dust has settled. The real users have moved in and the project is officially complete. It is actually *cool*. It looks good and seems to have a lasting quality that is indicative of good design.

The end-users praise the ease of use, effective technology, and improved productivity that is the outgrowth of a well-executed project. Their management thinks it is great too. They want to use it in promotions and public relations. They take photos and publish articles celebrating the excellence of the effort. Maybe it even wins an award (or two)!

Wisdom

However, there on the cover of the nation's leading industry trade magazine—taking center stage in the press coverage—is someone you barely remember. In fact, he was a minor supervisor or something, wasn't he? Now he is the project's *guru*.

He got a promotion after the departure of the original client visionary. He saw the flaws in the original concept and worked closely with a vendor (that you never heard of, or who was considered inappropriate by everyone during the design phase) to facilitate a new solution that clearly improved the original concepts (not really, but it makes good PR), and made this the project of a lifetime.

AT THE END OF THE DAY

Well, the anti-depressants have kicked in now. The project is over. It does not matter who gets credit because, at the end of the day it really was a job well done by all. Can you escape from this insidious pattern? Absolutely! All it takes is increased awareness, proactive communication, a focus on expertise, excellence, and experience, and maybe just small dose of humility. That is the moral of this tale.

The key to building an enduring practice is as simple as *expertise, excellence*, and *experience*. How you think about them, how you to sell them, and how you deliver to them will determine your success. Leadership, collaboration, and value are important elements to master if you are to be successful in designing, marketing, and growing your business. There are resources to help and there are many examples to follow. I believe you need to look outside the traditional paradigms of your sector of the professional service industry.

LEVERAGING YOUR **EXPERTISE**, CELEBRATING YOUR **EXCELLENCE**, AND DELIVERING **EXPERIENCE**, while seeking knowledge from the work of other creative enterprises can help you envision your dream practice, chart your course, and create an enduring destiny. Remember (to paraphrase the opening quote from Mr. Rickey): *"Luck is the residue of 'your' design!"*

The Architecture of Value

AFTERWORD

It's the end of the world as we know it (and I feel fine).
REM

AS YOU START TO THINK about how the elements of designing, marketing, and growing apply to your professional service firm, I end this book on a note of optimism. Occasionally the weight of experience causes me to reflect—with a slightly satiric view—on the reasons I chose to practice professionally in a project-oriented, service field. However, at the end of the day, I entered the service field for the satisfaction of seeing my efforts revealed in successful projects.

There is a certain unique satisfaction that comes from of your labors—the existential glow that occurs when you see the results of your hard work. I think that physical manifestation is one of the main reasons many of us continue to practice architecture—a field not known for financial reward, peer recognition, or fame.

On my first day as a student of architecture at California Polytechnic State University, San Luis Obispo, then Dean, George Haslin, FAIA, told the freshman class that if we had entered architecture for *wealth* to get out now—architecture has the lowest average income for a licensed professional. If we had entered for *recognition* by our colleagues, forget it—we would have to wait until we were 50 before other architects would consider us for the accreditation of Fellowship. Moreover, if we were in architecture for *fame*, it was probably not happening—ask your mother to name an architect other than Frank Lloyd Wright.

However, he also made one observation that is equally, if not more, important: *"Do what you love!"*

The Architecture of Value

While Dean Haslin's remarks were true, they did not dissuade me from pursuing my career path in architecture. Notwithstanding the many unexpected twists and turns my career has taken, the pleasure I have had working in the professional service industry has never diminished.

I believe, if you embrace the joy of *doing what you love*, you can succeed beyond your wildest dreams by focusing on designing, marketing, and growing your practice, and creating the foundation for an enduring professional service firm.

PERSONAL SATISFACTION COMES FROM THE REALIZATION that professional service is a team effort. Your choice of livelihood, views, thoughts, speech, actions, efforts, concentration, and mindfulness each contributes to your progress, to your firm's success, and to the success of your clients. In the end, the best you can do is stay on your chosen path, live by setting a good example, and work toward the goals of expertise-driven excellence and experience.

ENDNOTES

PART I | Design Your Practice

CHAPTER 1

1. Wilber, Ken, *A Theory of Everything: An Integral Vision for Business, Politics, Science and Spirituality*, Boston, MA: Shambala, 2001.

2. Paulson, Daryl, *Competitive Business, Caring Business*, San Francisco, CA: Paraview Press, 2002.

CHAPTER 2

3. Morgan, Nick, "How to Overcome 'Change Fatigue'," *Burning Questions 2001, A Special Report of the Harvard Management Update*, July 2001:2.

CHAPTER 3

4. Senge, Peter, *The Fifth Discipline: The Art & Practice of the Learning Organization*, New York, NY: Currency/Doubleday, 1994.

5. "Integrated Project Delivery—A Working Definition," *American Institute of Architects California Council*, May 15, 2007.

6. Yoder, Susan, "Bridging the Gap in Project Delivery," *PSMJ Project Delivery Quarterly No. 3*, Summer 1998: 8.

CHAPTER 5

7. Hochberg, Hugh and Dr. Ann Gardner, "The Archetypes of Leadership," presentation to the *American Institute of Architects* national conference, Dallas, TX, 1996.

CHAPTER 6

8. Kanchier, Carol, "To Be Successful, Mimic Successful People's Habits," *San Francisco Chronicle*, 5 August 2001.

9. Peters, Tom, "The Brand Called YOU!," Fast Company, August 1997: 83.

CHAPTER 7

10. McKenna, Regis, *Real Time: Preparing for the Age of the Never Satisfied Client*, Boston, MA: Harvard Business School Press, 1999.

11. Peppers, Don and Martha Rogers, PhD, *The One to One Future: Building Relationships One Client at a Time*, New York, NY: Currency/Doubleday, 1993.

12. Taylor, Jim and Watts Wacker, *The 500-Year Delta: What Comes After What Comes Next*, New York, NY: HarperBusiness, 1997.
13. Hiebeler, Robert, Thomas Kelly & Charles Kelly, *Best Practices*, New York, NY: Touchstone Books, 2000.
14. Rodin, Robert and Curtis Hartman, *Free, Perfect & Now: Connecting to the Three Insatiable Client Demands*, Carmichael, CA: Touchstone Books, 2000.

CHAPTER 8

15. Kelley, Tom, *The Art of Innovation: Lessons in Creativity from IDEO, America's Leading Design Firm*, New York, NY: Doubleday, 2001.
16. Flynn-Heapes, Ellen, *Creating Wealth: Principles & Practices for Design Firms*, Alexandria, VA: SPARKS: The Center for Strategic Planning, 2000.
17. Flynn-Heapes

CHAPTER 9

18. Peters, Tom, from speech given at the 45th *International Design Conference*, Aspen, Colorado, 1995.

CHAPTER 10

19. Maister, David, Charles Green and Robert Galford, *The Trusted Advisor*, Carmichael, CA: Touchstone Books, 2001.
20. Maister

CHAPTER 11

21. Robinson, Graham and Ellen Pothecary, "Designing and Building a World-Class Industry," Project Delivery Report, AIA Construction Management DesignBuild PIA, September, 1998: 8-12.
22. Robinson
23. Robinson
24. Peters, Tom, *Thriving on Chaos: Handbook for a Management Revolution*, New York, NY: Alfred A. Knopf, 1987.

CHAPTER 12

25. Faems, D., M. Janssens & B. Van Looy, "Inter-Organizational Collaboration to Develop New Technologies: Trust, Control, and Exploration," paper presented at *2nd Workshop on Trust Within and Between Organizations*, Amsterdam, October 23-24, 2003.

Endnotes

PART II | Market Your Practice

26. Nelson, Richard, formerly business development director with CRM SaaS providers, Cosential.
27. Rose, Stuart, Professional Development Resources.

CHAPTER 13

28. Levinson, Jay, *Guerilla Marketing: Secrets for Making Big Profits from Your Small Business*, Boston, MA: Houghton Mifflin, 1998.
29. Kawasaki, Guy, *How to Drive Your Competition Crazy: Creating Disruption for Fun and Profit*, New York, NY: Hyperion, 1996.
30. Kawasaki
31. Kawasaki
32. Wacker, Watts, Jim Taylor and Howard Means, *The Visionary's Handbook: Nine Paradoxes That Will Shape the Future of Your Business*, New York, NY: HarperBusiness, 2000.
33. Locke, Christopher, *Gonzo Marketing: Winning Through Worst Practices*, New York, NY: Perseus Press, 2001.

CHAPTER 14

34. Goldsmith, Andrew, "Here's an Idea That's Not Quite Ripe," *Fast Company*, October 1997: 50.
35. "Next Time, We Say Boil the Consultant," *Fast Company*, November 1995: 20.

CHAPTER 15

36. Burris, Daniel and Roger Gittines, *Technotrends: How to Use Technology to Go Beyond Your Competition*, New York, NY: HarperBusiness, 1994.
37. Handy, Charles and Warren Bennis, *The Age of Unreason*, Boston, MA: Harvard Business School Press, 1998.

CHAPTER 16

38. Rodin, Robert and Curtis Hartman, *Free, Perfect and Now: Connecting to the Three Insatiable Client Demands*, Carmichael, CA: Touchstone Books, 2000.
39. "Multi-Function CRM Software: How Good Is It," report by High-Yield Marketing & Mangen Research Associates, October 2001.
40. James, Geoffrey, "Underwhelmed," *Red Herring*, 12 July 2002.

The Architecture of Value

CHAPTER 17
41. Bennis, Warren, On Becoming a Leader, New York, NY: Perseus Publishing, 1994.
42. Senge, Peter, *The Fifth Discipline: The Art and Science of the Learning Organization*, New York, NY: Currency/Doubleday, 1994.

CHAPTER 18
43. Rose
44. Khalsa Mahan, *Let's Get Real or Let's Not Play: The Demise of Dysfunctional Selling and the Advent of Helping Clients Succeed*, New York: Franklin Covey, 1999)

CHAPTER 19
45. Pearson, Marjanne, from a moderated discussion on practice at the S*MPS Senior Marketer's Roundtable*, San Francisco, CA, January 2001.
46. Pearson
47. Pearson

CHAPTER 20
48. Reis, Al and Jack Trout, *Advertising Age*, 1972.

CHAPTER 21
49. Zeithaml, Valerie, A. Parasuraman and Leonard Berry, *Delivering Quality Service: Balancing Client Perceptions and Expectations*, New York, NY: Free Press, 1990.

CHAPTER 22
50. Gladwell, Malcolm, *The Tipping Point*, Boston, MA: Back Bay Books, 2002.
51. Godin, Seth, *Unleashing the Idea Virus*, Dobbs Ferry, NY: Do You Zoom, Inc., 2000.

CHAPTER 23
52. Stasiowski, Frank, "Creating High Impact Proposals," American Institute of Architects National Conference, San Francisco, June 1995.
53. Sanders, Janet, "Show & Sell: Communicate Winning Strategies, Structure, and Style," ACEC Marketing Summit, Newport Beach, CA, 18 January 2002.

Endnotes

CHAPTER 24

54. Selingo, Jeffrey, "A Message to Web Designers: If It Ain't Broke, Don't Fix It," *New York Times*, 3 August 2000: G11.

55. Kienle Communications and Sunbelt Research Associates, "National E-Technology Survey of Architecture, Engineering & Construction Companies," *SMPS Foundation Whitepaper*, August 2001.

56. Collins, James and Jerry Porras, *Built to Last: Successful Habits of Visionary Companies*, New York, NY: HarperCollins, 1994.

57. Park, Craig, "Accessing Online Services," *Systems Contractor News*, Volume 2, No. 3, March 1995.

58. O'Connor, James and Kelli Lieurance, "Social Networking and Email Policies in the Workplace," webinar by Baird Holm, Attorneys at Law, September 2009.

59. O'Connor and Lieurance

60. O'Connor and Lieurance

PART III | Grow Your Practice

61. Pine, Joseph and James Gilmore, *The Experience Economy*, Boston, MA: Harvard Business School Press, 1999.

CHAPTER 26

62. Pink, Daniel and Michael Warshaw, "The (Free-Agent) Declaration of Independence," *Fast Company*, December 1997, 152.

63. Woolridge, Adrian, "Come Back, Company Man," *New York Times Magazine*, 5 March 2000: 82.

64. Woolridge

65. Woolridge

66. Woolridge

CHAPTER 27

67. Negroponte, Nicholas, *Being Digital*, New York, NY: Random House, 1995.

CHAPTER 28

68. Lynch, Peter, *Beating the Street*, New York, NY: Simon & Shuster, 1993.

CHAPTER 29

69. Ellis, John, "Digital Matters," *Fast Company*, June 2001: 74.

70. Osborne, Cathy, "Enhancing Client Relationships: Moving from Client Lists to CRM Solutions," SMPS/CSMPS Regional Conference, Seattle, WA, October 2001.

CHAPTER 31

71. Stasiowski, Frank, "29 Terms to Include in A/E/P Contracts," *PSMJ Supplement*.

CHAPTER 32

72. Stasiowski, Frank, "10 Project Management Commandments," *PSMJ Supplement*.

CHAPTER 34

73. Mackay, Harvey, "Meet This Time-Gobbling Practice Head On," *San Francisco Chronicle*, 25 February 2001.

74. Paoletti, Dennis, "Flying with Eagles: An Interview with Peter Nosler, Co-Founder and CEO, DPR Construction," *SMPS Marketer*, April 1999.

75. Doyle, Michael and David Straus, *How to Make Meetings Work*, New York, NY: Berkley Publishing Group, 1993.

CHAPTER 37

76. Kane, Kate, "Are You Hyphen-ated Enough?" *Fast Company*, August 1996: 30.

BIBLIOGRAPHY

Bennis, Warren, *On Becoming a Leader*, New York, NY: Perseus Press, 1994.

Burrus, Daniel & Roger Gittines, *Technotrends: How to Use Technology to Go Beyond Your Competition*, New York, NY: Harperbusiness, 1994.

Collins, James & Jerry Porras, *Built to Last: Successful Habits of Visionary Companies*, New York, NY: Harperbusiness, 1997.

Doyle, Michael & David Straus, *How to Make Meetings Work*, New York, NY: Berkley Publishing Group, 1993.

Flynn-Heapes, Ellen, *Creating Wealth: Principles & Practices for Design Firms*, SPARKS: The Center for Strategic Planning, 2000.

Gladwell, Malcolm, *The Tipping Point*, Boston, MA: Little Brown & Company, 2000.

Godin, Seth, *Unleashing the Idea Virus*, Dobbs Ferry, NY: Do You Zoom, Inc., 2000.

Handy, Charles & Warren Bennis, *The Age of Unreason*, Boston, MA: Harvard Business School Press, 1998.

Hiebeler, Robert, Thomas Kelly & Charles Kelly, *Best Practices*, New York, NY: Touchstone Books, 2000.

Khalsa Mahan, *Let's Get Real or Let's Not Play: The Demise of Dysfunctional Selling and the Advent of Helping Clients Succeed*, New York: Franklin Covey, 1999)

Kawasaki, Guy, *How to Drive Your Competition Crazy: Creative Disruption for Fun and Profit*, New York, NY: Hyperion, 1996.

Kelley, Tom and David Kelly, *The Art of Innovation: Lessons in Creativity from IDEO*, New York, NY: Doubleday, 2001.

Levinson, Jay, *Guerilla Marketing: Secrets for Making Big Profits from Your Small Business*, Boston, MA: Mariner Books, 1998.

The Architecture of Value

Locke, Christopher, *Gonzo Marketing: Winning Through Worst Practices*, New York, NY: Perseus Press, 2001.

Lynch, Peter, *Beating the Street*, New York, NY: Simon and Schuster, 1993

Maister, David, Charles Green & Robert Galford, *The Trusted Advisor*, Carmichael, CA: Touchtone Books, 2001.

McKenna, Regis, *Real Time: Preparing for the Age of the Never Satisfied Client*, Harvard Business School Press, 1997.

Negroponte, Nicholas, *Being Digital*, New York, NY: Vintage Books, 1996.

Paulson, Daryl, *Competitive Business, Caring Business*, San Francisco, CA: Paraview Press, 2002.

Peppers, Don and Martha Rogers, PhD, *The One to One Future: Building Relationships One Client at a Time*, New York, NY: Currency/Doubleday, 1993.

Peters, Tom, *Thriving on Chaos: Handbook for a Management Revolution*, New York, NY: Alfred A. Knopf, 1987.

Peters, Tom, *The Pursuit of WOW!*, New York: Vintage Books, 1994.

Pine, Joseph and James Gilmore, *The Experience Economy*, Boston, MA: Harvard Business School Press, 1999.

Prosen, Bob, *Kiss Theory Good Bye: Five Proven Ways to Get Extraordinary Results in Any Company*, Dallas, Gold Pen Publishing, 2006

Rodin, Robert & Curtis Hartman, *Free, Perfect & Now: Connecting to the Three Insatiable Client Needs*, Carmichael, CA: Touchstone Books, 2000.

Senge, Peter, *The Fifth Discipline: The Art & Practice of the Learning Organization*, New York, NY: Currency/Doubleday, 1994.

Taylor, Jim & Watts Wacker, *The 500-Year Delta: What Happens After What Comes Next*, New York, NY: Harperbusiness, 1998.

Bibliography

Wacker, Watts, Jim Taylor with Howard Means, *The Visionary's Handbook: Nine Paradoxes That Will Shape the Future of Your Business*, New York, NY: Harperbusiness, 2000.

Wilber, Ken, *A Theory of Everything: An Integral Vision for Business, Politics, Science and Spirituality*, Boston, MA: Shambala, 2001.

Zeithaml, Valerie Zeithaml, A. Parasuraman & Leonard Berry, *Delivering Quality Service*, New York, NY: Free Press, 1990.

The Architecture of Value

OTHER RECOMMENDED READING

Goldratt, Eliyahu, *It's Not Luck*, North River Press, 1994.

Goldratt, Eliyahu, *The Goal*, North River Press, 1992.

Kanchier, Carole, PhD, *Dare to Change Your Job and Your Life*, Jist Works, 2000.

Kanter, Rosabeth Moss, *Evolve!*, Harvard Business School Press, 2001.

Kawasaki, Guy, Michele Moreno & Gary Kawasaki, *Rules for Revolutionaries*, Harperbusiness, 2000.

Kubal, Michael, Kevin Miller & Ronald Worth, *Building Profits in the Construction Industry*, McGraw-Hill, 2000.

Levinson, Jay, *Guerilla Selling*, Mariner Books, 1992.

Lipnack, Jessica & Jeffrey Stamp, *Virtual Teams*, John Wiley & Sons, 1997.

Mackay, Harvey & Ken Blanchard, *Swim with the Sharks Without Getting Eaten*, Ballantine Books, 1997.

Monahan, Marta, *The Courage to be Brilliant*, Vittorio, 2000.

Peters, Tom & Robert Waterman, *In Search of Excellence*, HarperCollins, 1982.

Peters, Tom, *The Circle of Innovation*, Vintage Books, 1999.

Peters, Tom, *The Professional Service 50*, Alfred A. Knopf, 1999.

Richter, Sam, *Take the Cold Out of Cold Calling*, Beaver's Pond Press, 2009.

SMPS, *Marketing Handbook for Design & Construction Professionals*, Building News International, 2009.

Whyte, David, *The Heart Aroused: Poetry and the Preservation of the Soul in Corporate America*, Currency/Doubleday, 1996.

The Architecture of Value

INDEX TO WEB LINKS

A
Advanced Management Institute | www.advancedmgmtinstitute.com
American Council of Engineering Companies (ACEC) | www.acec.org
American Institute of Architects | www.aia.org
Apple Computer | www.apple.com

B
Baird Holm | www.bairdholm.com
Barry, Barbara | www.barbarabarry.com
Bell, Patrick | www.patrickcbell.com
Black, Tracy | www.blackcapemarketing.com
Burrus, Daniel | www.burrus.com
Business by Design Solutions | www.businessbydesign.ca

C
California Polytechnic State University, San Luis Obispo | www.calpoly.edu/~caed/
Cisco Systems | www.cisco.com
Collins, Jim | www.jimcollins.com
Coxe Group | www.coxegroup.com
CRMGuru | www.crmguru.com

D
Deltek | www.deltek.com
Deming, W. Edwards | www.deming.org

DePree, Max | www.depree.org
Der Spiegel | www.spiegel.de
DPR Construction | www.dprinc.com
DuPuis, Stephen | www.dupuisgroup.com

E
eConnections | www.econnections.com
Economist | www.economist.com

F
Fast Company | www.fastcompany.com
Flynn-Heapes, Ellen | www.forsparks.com
Foster, Norman | www.fosterandpartners.com

G
Gartner Group | www.gartner.com
Gilmore, Jim | www.strategichorizons.com
Gladwell, Malcomb | www.gladwell.com
Global Design Alliance | www.globalda.com
Globe Street | www.globest.com
Goldratt, Eliyahu | www.goldratt.org
Google | www.google.com
Grove, Andy | www.andygrove.com

249

The Architecture of Value

H

Harvard Business Review | www.harvardbusinessonline.com/

I

IBM | www.ibm.com

IDEO | www.ideo.com

K

Kanchier, Dr. Carole | www.daretochange.com

Kanter, Rosabeth Moss | rosabethkanter.wordpress.com

Kawasaki, Guy | www.garage.com

L

Levinson, Jay | www.jayconradlevinson.com

Locke, Christopher | www.gonzomarketing.com

M

Mackay, Harvey | www.mackay.com

Maister, David | www.davidmaister.com

McGraw-Hill Construction | www.construction.com

McKenna, Regis | www.mckenna-group.com

Microsoft | www.microsoft.com

N

Negroponte, Nicholas | www.laptop.org

New York University | www.nyu.edu

Nielsen Norman Group | www.nngroup.com

Nike | www.nike.com

Nordstrom | www.nordstrom.com

O

1-to-1 Marketing | www.1to1.com

Oracle | www.oracle.com

P

Pearson, Marjanne | www.talentstar.com

Peters, Tom | www.tompeters.com

Popcorn, Faith | www.faithpopcorn.com

Porras, Jerry | www.jerryporras.com

Prosen, Bob | www.bobprosen.com

PSMJ Resources | www.psmj.com

R

Reilly, Michael | www.reillycommunications.com

Reis, Al | www.reis.com

Richter, Sam | www.samrichter.com

Rodin, Robert | www.econnections.com

S

Search Engine Watch | www.searchenginewatch.com

Senge, Peter | www.fieldbook.com

Silver, Dena and Charlie | www.msilverco.com

Society for Marketing Professional Services (SMPS) | www.smps.org

Sound & Video Contractor | www.svconline.com

SPARKS: The Center for Strategic Planning | www.forsparks.com

Index to Web Links

Stern, Robert A.M. |
www.ramsa.com

Stone Yamashita |
www.stoneyamashita.com

System Contractor News |
www.systemscontractor.com

T

Trout, Jack |
www.troutandpartners.com

U

University of Reading |
www.rdg.ac.uk

W

Wacker, Watts |
www.firstmatters.com

Wheatley, Margaret |
www.margaretwheatley.com

Y

Yahoo! | www.yahoo.com

Yuen, Cherri |
www.getcopywrite.com

The Architecture of Value

ACKNOWLEDGEMENTS

Find in middle air an eagle on the wing,
and recognize the five that make the muses sing.
William Butler Yeats

THERE ARE MANY PEOPLE WHO HELPED take my ideas from thought to paper, and without whom, this book would not exist. This third and retitled edition benefited from four decades of *learning by doing*. That experience, the lessons learned, confirmed my belief in the power and value of leadership, communication, and collaboration.

First, I thank the editors—Fred Ampel, David Keene, Kirsten Nelson, and Randy Pollock—of my originally published writing in *Sound & Video Contractor*, *Systems Contractor News*, and the SMPS *Marketer*. Their support of for publishing my views is the foundation of this book.

Special thanks go to Mike Reilly, Stacey Huscher, Marjanne Pearson, and Lisa Bowman for their editorial input to the first edition, and to attorney Gene Scheiman for his copyright review and confirmation that these same ideas could apply to any professional service.

A note of gratitude goes to my friends Mitch Levitt and Lee Slade, for the creating the concept *"Think. Sell. Deliver!"* as the tag line for the 2002 SMPS National Conference, *Get2Yes!* I admit I borrowed (read *"stole"*) that three-word premise and applied it to the original outline of this book.

This edition benefited greatly from the kind and informative editorial hand of Cherri Yuen of GetCopyWrite in its beginning, and Tracy Black, president of Black Cape Marketing, in its conclusion. Their encouragement, input, review, and content suggestions made this a much better book than I could have ever created alone.

The Architecture of Value

I am forever indebted to those mentors who have counseled me throughout my career—including Patrick Bell, Don Esters, Susan Harris, Marta Monahan, Susan Shippey, and Hubert Wilke—for their lasting influence.

Equally, I thank my closest friends—Barbara Barry, Scott Lindsay, Mike Savage, and Jerry Siebum, and especially, my sister, Leslie—who honor me with their enthusiastic and continued confidence.

And, I am forever thankful for the inspiration of that elusive muse who walks with me on the path for a *reason* or a *season*, and has given voice to my words for a lifetime.

FINALLY, TO MY SON, TREVOR, for your unconditional love, I dedicate this book. You make me a very proud father.

ABOUT THE AUTHOR

*In every man's writings, the character
of the writer must lie recorded.*
Thomas Carlyle

CRAIG PARK, FSMPS, ASSOCIATE AIA, has been active in the building industry for more than 40 years. He has held leadership positions in design, project management, marketing, business development, strategic planning, and operations.

Craig has worked for architects, engineers, contractors, and manufacturers in small and large firms. He has helped direct firms ranging from 20 to 650 people, spanning a single office to 25 branches and generating from $2M to $200M in revenue.

Craig holds a BS in Architecture from California State Polytechnic University, San Luis Obispo. He completed continuing post-graduate education studies at New York University (Microprocessor Technology) and the Advanced Management Institute for Architecture and Engineering in San Francisco (Leadership).

Craig is an associate member of the American Institute of Architects (AIA), and former national president of the Society for Marketing Professional Services (SMPS). The national Society honored Craig as a *Fellow* in 1993, a *Distinguished Life Member* in 2005, and in 2007 with the *Marketing Achievement Award* for his career accomplishments. The San Francisco/Bay Area SMPS Chapter presented him with the *William B. Hankinson Award for Lifetime Achievement* in 2005.

The Architecture of Value

Craig is the author more than 150 published articles on management, marketing, and technology. Craig's writing appears regularly in industry journals and newsletters, and he is a regular presenter at industry forums and conferences.

Craig wrote three chapters—*"Hiring Consultants and Managing Consultant Relationships," "The Use of Technology in Marketing,"* and *"Client Relationship Management"*— for the third edition of the *Marketing Handbook for Design and Construction Professionals* (BNi, 2009).

Craig also contributed the Foreword to Jerry Yudelson's *Marketing Green Building Services: Strategies for Success* (Architectural Press; 2007), and was featured in *I Should Be Burnt Out By Now, So How Come I'm Not?* (John Wiley & Sons; 2004) by Peg Neuhauser. He has presented at local, regional and national AIA, ACEC, IIDA and SMPS programs, among many others.

Craig's websites (*www.craigpark.com* and *www.thevirtualcmo.com*) provide information and resources for marketing, management, and leadership in professional practice.

Craig lives in Omaha, Nebraska. You can contact him at craig@craigpark.com.

www.ingramcontent.com/pod-product-compliance
Lightning Source LLC
Chambersburg PA
CBHW072131290426
44111CB00012B/1855